Conscious YOU
Conscious YOUth

How to Connect with Your Youth or Teen, while
Building Your Own Spiritual Ground.

TORI B. AMOS

BALBOA.
PRESS

A DIVISION OF HAY HOUSE

Illustrator credit for : Naima Eckhardt de Camargo

Balboa Press books may be ordered through booksellers or by contacting:

Balboa Press
A Division of Hay House
1663 Liberty Drive
Bloomington, IN 47403
www.balboapress.com
1 (877) 407-4847

Printed in the United States of America.

ISBN: 978-1-4525-9391-3 (sc)
ISBN: 978-1-4525-9392-0 (e)

Balboa Press rev. date: 1/19/2015

Contents

Chapter 2 Yoga and You

Chapter 3 Reiki Energy

Prologue

It is understandable that humanity is constantly trying to tweak and renew itself. It is also understandable that this type of human alignment is more easily done during the youthful or childhood years.

According to the particular child or youth, there will be different needs to consider. However, there are basic needs of youthful humanity. They are love, affection, attention, security, and guidance. These needs may also be met in later years of life. However, during the youthful years, the needs are more easily accomplished. Generally speaking, these needs may be considered physical, emotional or spiritual.

For over 5000 years, some of humanity, through different meditation modalities, have successfully empowered its youth. Since these needs are fundamental and universal, consider this: wouldn't it be wonderful if all of humanity could empower its youth with the spiritual and emotional fortitude to face the uncertainties of tomorrow?

Along with satisfying the basic needs, the empowered youth will have the patience and ability to relax and help themselves. That is the key, to help themselves! Wouldn't that be awesome? Within the pages of this book, there are some real answers. It is guaranteed!

A Child's Needs

A child needs love.

A child needs affection.

A child needs attention and not rejection.

A child needs direction.

A child needs care.

A child needs to know that you're always there.

A child needs discipline.

A child needs a smile.

A child needs to learn to feel worthwhile.

Brenda S. Amos, Ed D.

Creating a Space for a Youth to Meditate

Chapter notes for personal guide (support person)

Motivation for Personal Guide

Creating a Space for a Youth to Meditate is a "go to guide" for anyone who has a youth to love or parent. Because many of the meditations in the chapter are beneficial to all age groups, there are suggestions for all to explore.

This is a "how to guide" with tips, techniques, activities and interviews from people with different meditation backgrounds. These techniques are sure to have the youth of every age group and their personal guides "creating a space." Meditation is not only about creating a physical space but also finding the emotional and mental space, from within.

Today's world is fast paced. Social media, video games, texting, blogging, fast food and social activities, keep most families and kids on the run. This fast pace can overload brain waves, lead to hyperactivity, sleeping disorders, learning disorders and poor diets.

Such circumstances can often lead to poor grades, lack of emotional stability and self-control. It can also lead to illnesses and inappropriate behaviors, as well as arguing and low self- esteem. By offering a youth a chance to meditate, the necessary time is provided for unplugging and de-stressing. The youth can let go of worry from within and reconfigure the emotional self. By embracing this practice, meditation can be used to create and sustain a healthy and happy lifestyle.

Meditation expands the imagination and clears a path for the creative process. It clears emotional blocks and allows natural energy to flow. It is significant to note that for generations to come, this imagination and creativity will become a part of the process of technology and invention. Also in future times of struggle, this creative process will help support unity and peace.

It is beneficial for a personal guide to instruct and support a youth that is practicing meditation. This personal guide is a person who inspires confidence and also provides the training. When meditation begins, the challenge for the personal guide is to relax the youth. For at least the first few times, meditate with the youth. The more the personal guide and youth practice, together, the more confident and encouraged the youth will become to practice independently. Remember, mediation encourages a healthy imagination. It creates a gateway to a balanced life.

Rational

Creating a Space For a Youth to Meditate is like planting a seed, and then watching the seed grow and bloom into a glorious flower. The positivity (the result of the meditation) becomes the bee that collects the pollen, which creates positivity within the youth. This "positive bee affect" is something that is very special to see bloom within a practicing youth.

"The youth today are in such great need of support for the positive benefits that meditation has to offer."

According to the research from The David Lynch Foundation:

25% of teenagers suffer from anxiety disorders
6.5 million children struggle from disabilities that impair their ability to learn
One in four high school students have been offered, sold even given illegal drugs on school property
High stress levels also damage teachers and educators, resulting in an extremely high burnout rate
One in three children are either overweight or obese
Nearly 3 million children receive medication for ADHD

Quoted from the interview from Bob Roth, executive director of the David Lynch Foundation:

Bob Roth is the Executive Director of the David Lynch Foundation. He directed the initiative to begin and maintain Transcendental Meditation

(TM) programs. The programs are reaching over 250,000 at-risk students in 130 public and charter schools in the United States, Latin America, the Middle East and Africa.

He also serves as the national director of the Center for Leadership Performance, where he helps oversee the introduction of the TM program in business, industry, and governmental organizations. Mr. Roth has been a teacher of Transcendental Meditation for 40 years and is the author of the definitive book on this technique, fittingly titled, Transcendental Meditation. His book is published in 21 different languages.

Phone interview with Bob Roth June 2012

Q - "How do you think meditation, yoga, and Mindfulness practice helps children?"

A - Today's youth is experiencing extremely high levels of stress. Higher than any other time in the past. They are always plugged into the Internet, television, iphone, ipad, you know, just constantly "plugged in." The pressures, of school are very high.

Research shows youth as young as ten years old, even in the higher performing schools, can be experiencing levels of stress similar to the PTSD (post traumatic syndrome disorder) that soldiers experience overseas in combat. This high level of stress, absolutely undermines, not just the ability to learn, but also can cause depths of depression and anxiety, bipolar disorders plus learning disorders. This puts youth at risk for very difficult lives. This stress can sometimes lead to violence, high levels of substance abuse, high levels of suicide and crime. We have an epidemic of stress in society, and the conventional approach to handling these stresses, whether it's medical or pharmaceutical, can sometimes be quite dangerous.

Thankfully, some support as ancient as meditation and yoga are highly effective and noninvasive. They have no hazardous side effects. And far more effectively reduce stress in the lives of the young people than anything else that has ever been tried. The youth enjoy doing meditation and yoga in classrooms. This has come just in the nick of time, in my opinion. For humanity is in danger of losing an entire generation to stress and to the complications of stress.

Even beyond the stress, TM is proven to actually wake up the brain, so it's more than just a relaxation technique. It stimulates creativity and intelligence and decreases the effects of learning disabilities. It's not just a passive approach to relaxation. They call this "learning readiness," ready to learn and to absorb information. So TM has both sides going for it, reducing stress and waking up the brain and improving learning.

Q- What differences do you see in the children that are practicing TM? What boundaries are they pushing through, what are they doing that is different from other children that are not practicing TM? Are they more stress free? Are they getting higher grades?

A-It's across the board, a whole galaxy, of changes. One of the things is that the kids are happier, a level of stress is lifted off of them, and they are more like kids. They have higher self - esteem and they are happier with themselves. The research shows that as they are developing, they are using more of their brain and the test scores improve; the same with the grade point averages. Graduation levels improve, behavioral problems decrease. Also drug abuse, that is prevalent everywhere also decreases. Bullying, suspensions, expulsions and even dropouts have all decreased marginally.

And those are indicators, Tori that the conventional approaches can't touch; things are just sliding down and getting worse and worse. So it's very important that things are coming together quite naturally. That's why David Lynch has given scholarships to a quarter of a million kids, to teach average students to meditate and it is causing a significant difference in their lives.

Q- That is amazing Bob! So tell me more about TM meditation, I know that it uses Mantras.

A-The TM technique uses sound, there are meditations that are called Mantra meditations, but that doesn't mean they are all the same. TM uses a specific sound for the mantra, and the child is taught to use it in a unique way. The child isn't just taught how to just repeat it over and over again. The child is taught to use it easily and effortlessly for the body and mind to access what is already there, a profound rest. Deep within every human mind, no matter how frantic and noisy it may be on the surface, deep within everyone there is a level of the mind that is calm that is awake, like the deep silence under the depth of the ocean. So in the same way the mind is active on the surface, yet calm and wide-awake and powerful in its depths. And this meditation lets the students simply and effortlessly access that, the body gets deep rest, the mind wakes up, and all these wonderful things begin to take place.

And we use the Mantra or sound to access this to take place.

Tori -Excellent, ok!

Q-How do you feel that your schools are setting an example for other schools worldwide? I know, for example, the Mindful Life Project in Richmond, CA is a new non-profit organization, where more meditation is happening in school and healthy eating and things like this.

My daughter Mya is twelve and in the 7th grade, we live in Berkeley, CA and she goes to Martin Luther King Middle school. They have a very great system there, where students eat healthy! Alice Waters, the owner of Chez Panisse Restaurant in Berkeley, CA helped implement the Edible Schoolyard Project program at Martin Luther King, Jr.

Bob- I know all about that! I am a graduate of Berkeley, CA University. I know…!

Tori- Yes! Mya loves it and is doing well and is on the honor roll.

Q- So for these examples of programs being said, how is the David Lynch Foundation setting examples for schools worldwide?

A-I think that anytime a school is being visionary and practical in implementing yoga, healthy eating, and meditation, that school is knowingly or unknowingly, setting a model for all schools moving into the future. Because the mind-body approach to providing learning readiness is absolutely essential, the results are quite dramatic. When you look at San Francisco, there are over 2,000 kids in the public schools that learn TM along with their teachers twice a day, every day of the school year. All of our four schools are quiet at the beginning and the end of each school day and the whole school has quite time. The kids meditate, the teachers meditate, and in that restfulness at the beginning of the school day when they are done, their mind is wide, awake and ready to learn. And the research at the schools has shown that the grades have skyrocketed and at the end of the school day, they get rid of whatever stress they had during the day and calm themselves down so when they go home they are less likely to act out, say and do stupid things, like take drugs. It's a model just as you put it Tori. They are model schools for the 21st century.

This is a key point; education has to go beyond information-based education, which is simply cramming a kid's brain full of facts. They can't handle it; they are too young to handle that kind of input. It overwhelms them, stresses them out and leaves them unhappy and unbalanced. Consciousness based approaches - the yoga and meditation based approach, we call it the consciousness approach to education. It's the foundation to all learning, because when the brain is settled and the mind is settled and alert, the child is happy. It only takes a few minutes at the beginning and end of each school day. The brain of the student can absorb all the information, to be used to the best of their ability.

Q- What age is appropriate in starting TM?

A-We start around the age of eleven or twelve; sometimes we start a little younger.

Q- I believe you mentioned this. But how do you see it fit to have these practices, like Reiki, meditation and yoga in the schools. Twice a day?

A-Yes with TM they call it quiet time. Kids are in their chairs for their first period class, the bell gets rung, and for about 10 -15 minutes the whole school is quiet. It's unbelievable. And the whole school moves into a deep state of restfulness. And after those 10 – 15 minutes, the child opens his or her eyes. Then the teacher starts teaching. Research shows that if the child is hyped, tweaked or buzzed, the teacher can try to get all the information into or out of them, but their mind is not as ready.

Q- How are the teachers, parents and staff affected by this program in the schools as well?

A-When we go into schools, all of the teachers, parents, and staff are offered to practice TM. A lot of the times the parents are doing TM at home or in their offices. You can go to www.david lynch foundation. com. There are a lot of pictures of the children meditating. I think the main thing on this Tori, is if you change the way of education, you have to have that change, produce positive results. It can't just be a person's experience. The lovely thing about these quiet times and TM, is there is a lot of independent research that shows just how significant the changes are, and not just from one school but all of the schools all across the country and all over the world.

Tori – That's amazing!

Q- What makes you so excited Bob, doing the good work that you do?

A-When I was a student at University CA, Berkeley, I was an education major and working on curriculum devolvement when I learned to meditate, way back when I was 18 years old between my freshman and sophomore year. I first had this experience and was thinking I would like to teach this to young students. And the year 1972, I became a teacher of TM; I studied with Maharishi Mahesh Yogi, the founder of TM, who actually introduced it to the world.

So over the last 40 years I have been teaching to housewives and husbands. The last seven years with the David Lynch Foundation we have been offering TM to entire schools. You know the experience I had 40 years ago just grew stronger and never left me. So this is very fulfilling for me to see this happening everywhere!

Q-Ok wonderful! That was actually my next question. What is your reward? I think for you that your reward is just spreading the word and it's part of what you have been wanting to do for a big part of your life.

A-Yes. Like you Tori, and so many of us, I was raised that I should go out and make a difference in the world and that I should give back. And I am fortunate to give back whatever I have received, like this knowledge. My parents raised me this way; it's my responsibility to give back.

My reward is when one's cup runs over and one is filled up from the meditation practice and a healthy way of life, a productive way of life is attained. It's very joyful, as you know Tori. Then to turn it around and offer it to others there are no words to describe how satisfying it is to see that the work at David Lynch Foundation and that all the good things that are being done. It's the quiet time program, not just quiet time that counts! We are also working with veterans and prisoners, inmates and guards, shelters, Native American reservations, women and girls that have been victims of abuse and torture and rape in Africa and Asia. So I am just bursting with happiness, to be able to do what I get to do.

Tori- That is wonderful and well said. Me too, I am so happy to be working with families and children and my own daughter, Mya. I taught Mya Reiki and she loves it.

Bob – Oh yeah you must love it and you share my experience, Tori, you do.

Tori- Yes and people ask me about my lifestyle and the "cross training" of the Mind Body and Awareness method that I use and live by. And many people ask me "why don't you write it down and show me or show my child, or my cousin."

Bob – Yes exactly, all these things are necessary. It is exercise not just from the standpoint of the mind and body, not just diet or service, it's everything. For a whole, integrated healthy life.

Tori- Yes a whole integrated lifestyle is essential and this is the emphasis actually the core of what I am writing about, in my book, "Conscious You Conscious Youth ," for children and everyone. For a quick example of an activity, in the book, yes, we can do yoga for exercise, but there are other exercises out there. For instance, you can jog, hula-hoop, jump rope etc. and what other exercises can you do? Yes, you can eat a healthy salad or snack, but what other healthy foods can you eat? Let the kids fill in the blanks too, to get their minds going on the healthy track. And have a suggestion key for them. For example take a Zumba class or practice TM. They may know of some ways they can fill in the blanks and learn something new, as well.

So I am really happy to be putting all this together for the youth and reaching out to you and other organizations to get everyone's input that I can, and put it all together. I am writing a self - help first beginners guide for children and those who will support and love them through their process.

So that hopefully when they become adults they already have the sustainability and the consciousness in them that they won't get into different problems down the road. If they do, we know this is life, however, they will be better equipped and have the tools they need to deal with life's challenges a bit better.

Bob- Yes! I have to say you are a noble soul and doing a great service to the next generation and the next generations too.

Tori- Thank You!

Benefits of Meditation

Meditation creates stillness, a time to be centered within the mind and emotions. It creates consciousness and teaches youth strong self-help techniques. The youth will have better relationships at home; have better sleeping patterns and experience less peer pressure. This encourages the youth to be self-supportive and creates a more independent, self-sufficient adult.

The future will reflect an adult who is self-sufficient in relationships, finances, and education. The ability to acquire the capacity to deal with reality and not be pulled in too many directions will definitely develop. For "knowing who we are, really" in this world is essential!

Physically speaking, the youth who works out on a regular basis has improved cardiovascular health, strength and agility. Also, research shows that certain basic mechanisms of the mind, for example attention, can also be trained and improved through systematic practices such as meditation. There are many forms and types of meditation. This book can help guide you to the ones that are right for you and the youth in your life.

Q & A with J.G. Larochette of the Mindful Life Project

Q: How has meditation helped your life?

A: Mindfulness has helped me tremendously in my life!! It has given me the gift of the present moment and how to find it without judgment, gently, with great compassion and kindness. I am able to redirect my thoughts, feelings, and emotions away from the future or the past and feel the power of this all-important moment we have in the "Now." Before mindfulness I often found myself getting attached to my emotions and now I am able to notice them and watch them flow by. It has given me the opportunity to live each moment as a brand new one, which of course it is!

Q: How long have you been meditating?

A: I started meditating two and half years ago and have been practicing mindfulness (a form of meditation) for the last two years.

Q: Why do you recommend it to people?

A: I recommend mindfulness for so many reasons!!! The awareness and ability to see life in the present moment and through a specific non–judgmental lens brings the opportunity to improve oneself at all times. We often live our life thinking or feeling things that happened in the past or the will happen in the future, but mindfulness gets us back to all that matters, THE PRESENT! The power, that being in the present moment brings, is an ability to live each moment fully, with compassion, love and interconnectedness.

Q: Tell me about your work in schools.

A: When I started in education at the ripe age of 22 at Play Works (then called Sports4Kids) I only knew I loved kids and sports. The past 10 years in education have brought me on a journey from play and sports to presence and mindfulness. At Play Works I learned the tools and skills to create a playground environment of respect and fun.

Despite working at very rough schools, fights, referrals, and negative behavior dramatically decreased. From this experience, I saw the need for that same healthy environment in the classroom. I became a teacher, bringing the fun back to learning. The students responded well with discipline, respect, excitement and most of all happiness.

A couple years ago, however, I began to see a change in my students. The kids were disconnected from themselves and the world. They lacked self-esteem, imagination and love of life. I re-evaluated the way I was supporting students. Why couldn't I engage the students as well as before? The students were dealing with similar life experiences, yet they were less present. I dedicated myself to living and learning through personal healing and empowerment and I invited my students to go on this journey with me. I took mindfulness classes through Mindful Schools and used the curriculum in my classrooms—yoga, play, art, positive hip-hop and more. The students responded immediately and the result has been amazing.

As the school climate continued to be chaotic, my students were in the "eye of the storm." I now realize, just as Jill Vialet did with Play Works, the power of guiding kids to find the power within them. By doing this, opportunities open for their personal success. Students understand that life can be most trying and challenging. These moments create strength and resiliency.

This sparked a deep passion in my heart, and I created the Mindful Life Project to reach the most "at – risk" behavioral problems at school. The students learn proven skills, that allow them to detach from the emotions and feelings that have been controlling their lives. They come to the realization that they can always find the inner greatness that they have. They can stop the cycle of negative thoughts and behavior and redirect the energy to positive choice making and empowerment. The goal is to always be present and open to the moment and to the flow of life. Mindful Life Project starts with the hope that we, as a society, can become supportive of all our children and start to reach the needs we have, one child at a time.

Q: What type of meditation and mindfulness do you practice? And teach?

A: I practice mindfulness in a very particular and specific way that allows me to observe my body, my senses, my mind and my connection to the people and the world around me. This is also the way we teach our students.

Q: How do you teach this and to whom?

A: Mindful Schools in Oakland, CA created our core mindfulness curriculum. We teach it for approximately 20 minutes at a time in a very sequential and guided way. We have taught over 1,100 kindergarteners through 8th graders in West Contra Costa County. We have worked with five elementary schools and two middle schools.

Q: How often do you meditate and suggest children to have "quiet time?"

A: I have mindful sits every day for about 20-30 minutes. I recommend that children start with five minutes a day, and then strengthen their practice. Slowly they will get to a time that is comfortable and brings them a deep connection that allows deep concentration, awareness and mental strength. I see it in a similar way as when we are getting strong muscles. You can't be the strongest person in the world in just one day. It takes much practice. The mind is similar and it is something that needs to be trained over long periods of time.

Q: How do you describe the program that you provide?

A: Mindful Life Project is a program that was created to empower students to the highest level possible. We build on the student's strengths and guide them in finding the tools and skills that already reside deep in their being. We want children to know that they are very talented, gifted and resilient. Our instructors work with great passion to guide students with love, compassion, and respect!

Q: How does it affect and benefit the children as they grow into their adult lives?

A: This is a great question. We won't know the full effect yet, as our students are still young, but we believe that when taught skills and tools that build self-regulation, confidence, and resilience that they will know that the world is full of possibilities. They can achieve anything if they put their heart and mind to it!

Q: What do you feel about the importance, of the "Cross Training" of mindfulness for the youth?

Example: Mindfulness, Healthy Diet, Meditation and Reiki

A: It is so important that our youth are taught all aspects of living a healthy and prosperous life. Our society has many unhealthy lifestyle opportunities and children tend to be guided in that direction. The need to be given healthy living tools including diet, mindfulness, energy healing and a consistent physically active lifestyle.

Q: Tell me about the yoga studio that you are opening in Richmond, CA.

A: Mindful Life Yoga is a way for us to bring wellness to the adult community while benefiting the work we do at Mindful Life Project. It is constant revenue stream that funds the work we do at underserved schools that don't have the resources to pay fully for our services. We are hopeful to build community, awareness and an opportunity for people to benefit their own health and the health of the kids in our partner schools.

Q: What else can you tell me about the Mindful Life Project?

A: Mindful Life Project was something that I started from the deepest most spiritual and loving place. I hope that our organization is around for a long time to come! It is with great honor and excitement that I am reporting that three of our partner schools had significant increases in their academic performance in the 2012-2013 school year. Richmond College Prep is one of the most amazing educational institutions I have ever seen. Visionary Ms. Peppina Chang, reached an 828 API, passing the state's proficiency level of 800, leads the school. We are so grateful to all of our partner schools and are looking forward to teaching mindfulness to over 1,400 South Richmond, CA students at five partner schools in the 2013-2014 school year. This includes our small group intervention program "Rise –Up" that will be at all five school sites and our "Mindful Community" program that will be at three sites.

August 29th 2013

----End chapter notes---

Why Meditation?

You don't' have to wait in line! It's free! It's freeing! Madonna and Oprah are doing it! No RX needed! No harmful side effects! Pop Culture's finest are doing it, too! It's better than a book and better than a movie! Even better than chocolate! It's fantastic! Schools are doing it too! International airports and hospitals are doing it! Those who attend Yoga centers are doing it! And you can learn to do it too! It's Mediation!!

History of Meditation

Meditation is an ancient practice of relaxing the mind and body. This practice started about 5000 years ago in India. Meditation began as a system of yoga principles. The Brahmin priests orally passed down these principles by making them into chants. Sites in Indus Valley, India dating back to 3000 BC have figures in yoga meditation poses.

Buddha is one of the history's most prominent figures and major icons of meditation. He first made his mark in 500 BC. His teaching spread far and wide across Asia. Many countries and cultures began to adopt meditation practices and their ideas of the word. They found their own unique ways of meditation practices.

Thousands of years after the beginning of meditation with the Brahmin priests, many forms of meditation began to take form. The practice of meditation spread to the west. It began to gain popularity in the twentieth century. In the 1960's and 1970's many professors and researchers began to study the practice of meditation and found its many benefits.

Jordan

Creating a Space for a Youth to Meditate

Be more of a trendsetter than a follower! Be thoughtful! Be a positive lifestyle's advocate! The connection will quickly and easily be made to the objective of "holding conscious space for a youth." In essence, there are six stages in Creating a Space for a Youth to Meditate. It is a time for the personal guide to connect with the youth, creating the environment for Conscious YOU, and the Conscious YOUth, to begin and grow.

These categories will be applicable to all of the ten types of meditation covered in this chapter.

Six categories to Creating a Space for a Youth to Meditate

- The Willingness to Participate / Desire
- The Space
- The Idea
- The Mood
- The Time
- The Routine

Julianna

1. The Willingness to Participate / Desire

Encourage the youth, but be sensitive to circumstances. See where the youth is mentally and emotionally at the time. Applaud the youth for their participation.

2. The Space (for most meditations)

Have a clean and clutter free space. A room with a comfortable temperature, the less noise the better. Provide a comfortable chair or pillow. Put on some calming music and light some candles, if appropriate.

3. The Idea

Ease into the meditation one step at a time.

Tell the youth, "It's almost time for our quiet time" Or " It's almost time to meditate." Or create your own words to let the youth know that the meditation will soon begin.

4. The Mood

Select the meditation or music that you enjoy. Dim the lights to begin relaxation.

5. The Time

Try every morning or before bedtime. Whatever time works best.

6. The Routine

Try to use the same time of day or night. Every day is preferable, or at least 4-5 times a week.

Why Meditation?

Children are tomorrow's leaders and need our support, love, and guidance today! How can we bridge the gap? One way is by using the powerful tool of meditation!

Meditation and the awareness of breath allow the youth to empty the mind and clear out the mind-chatter. This helps to remove any thoughts that do not serve. Having peace and the unity of the mind will propel the youth's positive passions and will guide powerful inner thoughts.

Refocusing the mind on goals and dreams, plus being present in the now moment is cultivated by meditation. Becoming aware of your own presence in the world is important. Meditation can catapult the youth from ordinary to extraordinary!

Elias

Meditation Begins

Before meditating, it may take up to five minutes to quiet the mind-chatter. Try to meditate 15 - 20 minutes, twice a day. Suggested times are in the morning or right before bedtime. You may sit up or slightly recline. Just remember that it's not naptime!

Possible dialogue to beginning meditation and the mindset:

Go beyond the mind-chatter. Hear your own thoughts and let them guide you. These thoughts makeup your inner voice. Your inner voice may come to you in a quiet whisper. This voice is your inner compass that guides you to do what is right and mindful. It also is a warning to warn you of something harmful that may be happening and to protect yourself from it.

So, go beyond this mind-chatter. In other words, go beyond the other thoughts and sounds that you may be hearing in your mind. To make it easier, you can pretend that you have cotton in your ears.

Now, go beyond the sounds of people and things that are physically around you at the time. And let the silence and peace seep in….

Can you "picture this?" There is a space in between the stars. Some people say it is where information is sent and received. You are under the cover of the moonlight, gazing at the twinkling stars.

You are embraced and supported by the clouds and are roaming around with the wind. You have your own inner star illuminating, shining... guiding your own path. You have your own wind giving power to your own inner sails. You are entering into meditation; quiet time. Here you can listen, create, open, renew, awaken and understand.

Now, you may feel hot or cool, light as a feather, or as heavy as an oak tree. These are all good and fine. You are there. And it is your time to relax and unwind. After a time, you will begin to stop meditating and regain your here and now.

Ready Set Go!

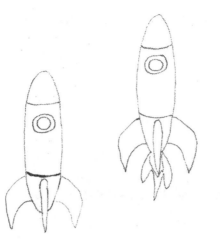

1- Ordinary (still on ground) 2- Extraordinary (taking off)

Ten Styles of Meditation:

There are different types of meditation. Some types relate to age groups, some relate to preferences. There is a meditation that is suited for all age groups.

1. Color Meditation: 2- 4+ years old

Pull out the crayons, paints, pastels or markers. Choose the medium you would like to use. Guides may choose the same colors and mediums that youth chooses, as well.

The guide may want to mirror the youth's splatters and squiggles. This mirroring creates a bond between the guide and the youth. The idea is to receive positive attention, encourage creativity and expand the imagination.

Key Points:

- Bonding
- Using self expression
- Expanding creativity and imagination
- Color Therapy

2. Mindful Meditation: 7 - 9+ years old

This is the practice of focusing on the present moment. Mindful Meditation allows you to become more aware of yourself and others. It also helps you become aware of your immediate surroundings.

Practicing non-judgmental attention to the details of your current reality is the focus; not escaping from your reality. Perhaps you have had a hard time staying happy. Do you translate this hard time into worry or fear? Do you fear that happiness won't last? Do you try to keep happiness from fading away?

Because of the awareness of the situation at hand, focus on the "here and now." This helps you to move through challenges more easily. You will learn to understand yourself and how to fit into your present surroundings. This will encourage you to keep a fresh outlook on life, moment-to-moment.

You will develop an understanding that what is going on "right now," is not going to change immediately. It is already happening. But in the still moments of Mindful Meditation, you will find a way for an uncomfortable situation to unfold into a comfortable one.

Know that sometimes, you can control your conditions. Know also, that sometimes you can't. However, you can learn to always control your response to the conditions.

#1 Activity:

For 60 seconds with your eyes open, focus on your breath and just breathe in and out. When thoughts arise in your mind and they will… practice letting the thoughts go.

#2 Activity:

Without thinking of anything, close your eyes and count from one to ten. If your mind starts to - wander and you begin to think of something, let go of the thought. Begin back at one, until you can count from one to ten with no thoughts.

Hint:

NO: "One, two, three, I wonder what's for dinner?" four, five, six…

Yes: One, two, three, four, five, six, seven, eight, nine, ten….

While you are sitting and focusing, Mindful Meditation nurtures you. You can also bring movement to your meditation as well.

Key Points:

- Practicing Mindfulness improves both mental and physical health.
- If the sitting meditation is not comfortable, try a mindful movement meditation, such as yoga.
- Mindfulness involves acceptance and concentration. It involves you becoming aware of thoughts and sensations without judgment.
- Mindful meditation scientifically has been found to be one of the key elements of happiness.

3. Focused Meditation: 7 - 9 + years

Focused meditation is very similar to Mindful meditation. However, with focused meditation, you focus by using one or more of your five senses: smell, taste, sight, sound and touch. This may be the easiest meditation of them all because you just focus on one of the senses.

You see, the idea is to bring awareness to one of the senses in order to engage in the present moment. For example, focus on a sound (bells) or a smell (rose) or a visual piece (a pleasing picture.) Focused meditation invites you not to think, but to simply experience the present moment.

Activity:

Sitting with your eyes opened or closed practice #1 Activity or #2 Activity of the Mindful meditation. Add in some "brain booster" sounds to enhance to meditation. There are "brainwave boosters" for creativity, memory, mental refresher, studying, concentration, whole brain functioning and more. Brain boosters enhance memory and intelligence as well as improving mental functions.

Note: You can find brain booster meditations and sounds online and at your local library.

"Read aloud"

During this focused meditation, you will focus on your breath. This will calm your mind and relax your body. There is no right or wrong way to meditate. Whatever you experience during this breathing meditation is right for you. Don't try to make anything happen; just observe.

Begin by finding a comfortable position, but one in which you will not fall asleep. Sitting on the floor with your legs crossed is a good position to try.

Activity:

Close your eyes or focus on one spot in the room.
Roll your shoulders slowly forward and then slowly back.
Lean your head from side to side, lowering your left ear toward your left shoulder and then your right ear toward your right shoulder.

Relax your muscles.

Your body will continue to relax as you meditate.

Observe your breathing. Notice how your breath flows in and out. Make no effort to change your breathing in any way, simply notice how your body breathes. Your body knows how much air it needs. Take a few deep belly breaths. Your belly will expand on inhales (breathing in) and relax during exhales (breathing out).

Sit quietly, seeing in your mind's eye your breath flowing gently in and out of your body.

When your attention wanders, as it will, just focus back again on your breathing.

Notice any stray thoughts, but don't dwell on them. Simply let the thoughts pass.

See how your breath continues to flow...deeply... calmly.

Notice the stages of a complete breath... from the inhale... to the pause that follows... the exhale... and the pause before taking another breath... See the slight breaks between each breath.

Feel the air entering through your nose or mouth...picture the breath flowing through the cavities in your sinuses or throat and then down to your lungs...

As thoughts intrude, allow them to pass and return your attention to your breathing.

(Pause)

Feel the air inside your body after you inhale, filling your body gently. The space inside of your lungs actually becomes smaller after you exhale and the air leaves your body.

Feel your chest and stomach gently rise and fall with each breath.

Now as you inhale, count silently... one

As you exhale, count...one

Wait for the next inhale, count again... one

Exhale...one

Inhale...one

Exhale...one

Continue to count each inhalation and exhalation as "one."

You have one continuous breath that flows without interruption.

(Pause)

Notice now how your body feels.

See how calm and gentle your breathing is and how relaxed your body feels.

Now it is time to gently reawaken your body and mind.

Keeping your eyes closed, notice the sounds around you. Feel the floor beneath you. Feel your clothes against your body.

Wiggle your fingers and toes.

Shrug your shoulders.

Open your eyes and remain sitting for a few moments longer.

Straighten out your legs and stretch your arms and legs gently.

Sit for a few moments more, enjoying how relaxed you feel and experiencing your body's reawakening and your mind returning to its usual level of alertness.

Slowly return to a standing position and continue with the rest of your day, feeling re-energized.

Key Points

- Reduces stress
- Improves memory and attention
- Increase creativity and feelings of compassion
- Use of your five senses

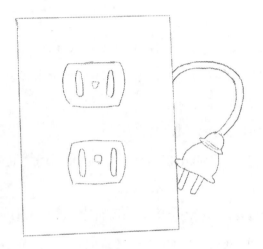

4. Guided Meditation: 5 - 7+ years

Guided meditation is simply meditation with the help of a guide. The guide can be a person, or a pre-recorded meditation. It's one of the easiest ways to reduce stress and enter into a state of deep relaxation, inner stillness, and positive personal change.

The guide or the recording will encourage relaxation and continue on to lead through a series of visualizations. You gradually relax and your mind becomes more and more clear. Many times, guided meditations are designed for empowerment, positive thinking and overall self-love.

The meditation is effortless! What is needed is to just relax and listen. Afterwards, there will be a feeling of empowerment and positive thinking!

Activity for the Child and the Guide:

Guided Meditation (ten minutes)

Read aloud:

You are encouraged to close your eyes, but for the first few times, open is OK. Your eyes may close later on in the meditation. Sit quietly for as long as possible. This is a great way to begin the practice of meditation.

Take three deep breaths, in and out of your nose.

Sitting comfortably and quietly, become aware of your breath. If you hear any outside noise, let it come and then go. Feel your heart beat. Feel your chest rising and falling as you breathe. Take a moment to feel the rhythm of your heart and breath as they create the music that sustains you.

Feel your heart and your breath. Your chest rising and falling.

You are loved, you are perfect, you are special, you are treasured, and you have time right now for yourself.

Imagine yourself in nature, in a meadow, surrounded by tall green grass with the warm earth under you, or by the ocean, with the warm grainy sand under your feet as you hear the rhythm of the waves.

You can create your own space in your mind, be there! Imagine the sun shining down on your skin. Feel the glow of the warmth filling you up in the sunshine.

Breathe in the warmth and the white yellow glow of the sun. You are feeling safe and warm. Feel the breeze blowing by. Hear the sound of your breath as your chest rises and falls. This is your safe space, your safe, feeling place. This space is yours. Breathe it in.

You are always safe here. In this space you can send love to family and friends. You can feel the love that they send to you. Now feel the white yellow light from the sun surrounding you. Feel the light going out to the earth and feel the love coming back to you.

Feel connected to this space as you breathe in deeply. Feel your heartbeat. Feel your chest rise and fall. Your body is warm and full of light. Nothing from without can touch this perfect light within you. The warm yellow white light warms your heart and you feel light and flowing. Nothing can touch you that you do not create. Stay here, breathe here, love and be safe here.

When you are ready, open your eyes, come back to the now moment.

Key Points:

- It's effortless
- It's a stress- buster

5. Transcendental Meditation (TM) 5+ years

Transcendental Meditation, sometimes called (TM) is an ancient form of meditation for effortless transcending. TM is a meditation practice that uses mantras. Mantras are words or phrases used in repetition to create focus and to free the mind. A mantra that is suited for you is chosen by your certified TM guide/instructor. TM is practiced 15-20 minutes, twice a day, while sitting comfortably.

TM brings you to a higher level within yourself; it offers you the most time for silence and peace. During this peaceful time, a time of restful alertness, your brain functions are significantly greater. You have a greater bond with your mind, body and awareness.

With TM your body benefits from a period of deep rest. More than any other meditation, TM has proven to be twice as effective in reducing stress, managing high blood pressure and anxiety.

Note: TM is very personal to everyone. It is recommended that you find a Transcendental Meditation center in your local area to work with you.

Key Points:

- Reduces Stress
- Creates a positive individual that can be a great help in their community, society and the world
- Enhances creativity

- Increase full brain potential creating a higher IQ and academic performance
- Reduces high blood pressure
- Strengthens communication in the brain waves and brain functions

6. Movement Meditation: 0+ years

Is the art of meditating while in motion. Here are five examples of movement meditation. The form you choose will be truly unique to you!

Hint: If you have a previous condition, check with your physician before engaging in the following movement meditations. With any movement meditation it is always best to warm up, first.

❖ Tai Chi: 4+years

"The belief system of Tai Chi is that you don't need to subscribe to or learn much about its roots. This is a Chinese philosophy. Tai Chi is a system of slow meditative physical exercise designed for relaxation, balance and health. Many enjoy its health benefits, movement and technique. Tai Chi uses the ideas of Qi and yin and yang."

"Qi- An energy force thought to flow through the body. Tai Chi is said to unblock and encourage the proper flow of Qi."

"Yin and yang - Opposing elements thought to make up the universe, that needs to be kept in harmony. Tai chi is said to promote this balance."

Quoted from Harvard Health Publications

Tai Chi is a hard and soft martial arts practice. "The soft and the pliable will defeat the hard and strong." This is a quote from the Tai Chi practice. It is known for its slow and focused movements. There is a slow and rhythmic motion to Tai Chi. Your body tells a story through its movements and hand positions.

Activity: Locate a local Tai Chi gathering. You can also find many videos online. This practice is great for optimizing your health for medical conditions as well.

Key Points:

- Muscle strength
- Flexibility
- Balance
- Cardio Strengthening
- Optimizing Health

❖ Yoga 0+ years

(See Yoga and You Chapter)

Many people who practice yoga do so to maintain their health and well being, improve physical fitness, relieve stress and enhance the quality of life. In addition, yoga is also used to address specific health conditions, such as back pain, neck pain, arthritis and anxiety.

Activity: Locate a local yoga studio that teaches the style of yoga you enjoy.

Key Points:

- Reduces Stress
- Reduces Physical Pain
- Creates Relaxation
- Better Rest
- Flexibility
- Increases Well Being

❖ Walking Meditation 5-6 years +

Keep your eyes open and walk. Very simple! Be mindful of your steps. As you walk along, be mindful of objects and people that maybe in your way. Take the time to notice your body and how it moves. If you move at a faster pace, notice an increase in your breathing. Taking a few deep breaths as you walk, knowing that the earth is holding you up, you are not holding up yourself! Take in the elements that may be surrounding you, the sun, the wind, and the rain. Also hear sounds of people, animals and cars. But, no matter what you may come across, always focus on your gentle steps and your breath.

Key Points:

- Exercise
- Sleep Better and Feel More Rested
- Your body becomes more flexible and you improve your overall health
- Cardio Conditioning

❖ Taekwondo 3-6+ years

Taekwondo is one of the world's most popular martial arts. It's so popular it's an event in the Summer Olympics. Translated means " the way of the fist foot." It is similar to karate and uses a series of kicking techniques. The reason for this technique is that the leg is stronger than the arm and has a longer reach. The art originated in Korea. This is a wonderful movement meditation for those that don't like to sit for too long. Taekwondo uses both physical and mental strength.

Key points, quoted from, What are the Benefits of Taekwondo for Kids? Global Post

Key Points:

- Physical Strength and Balance
- Coordination
- Concentration
- Breathing and Meditation Techniques
- Focus
- Discipline and Respect
- Self- confidence
- Personal Progress and Increasing Mastery of the Art
- Reduced Aggression

Activity: Find a local Taekwondo studio in your area. Take a class and see if this martial art is for you.

❖ Qigong (Chi Kung) 1+

Qigong is made up of two Chinese words. Qi is pronounced "chee" and is usually translated to mean the life force or vital-energy that flows through all things in the universe.

The second word, Gong, pronounced "gung", means accomplishment, or skill that is cultivated through steady practice. Together, Qigong means cultivating energy, it is a system practiced for health maintenance, healing and increasing vitality. Qigong is an integration of breathing techniques, physical postures and focused intentions.

There are many great things about the practice of Qigong. One is that it is slow and gentle and can be practiced by all age groups and even the physically challenged. Qigong practices can be classified as medical, martial or spiritual. All styles have three things in common: posture, (whether moving or stationary), breathing techniques, and mental focus. Some practices, increase the Qi; others circulate it, use it to heal and cleanse the body, store it or emit Qi to help heal others. Practices vary from external vigorous styles such a Kung Fu, or soft internal styles such as Tai Chi.

Qigong is gentle and rhythmic. It's great appeal is that everyone can benefit, regardless of ability, age, belief, or life circumstance.

Key Points:

- Children learn to channel their energy and develop increased concentration
- Reduces stress
- Improves cardiovascular, respiratory, circulatory, lymphatic and digestive functions

Activity: Find a local Qigong center and or check online for videos.

Note: The more you use your chi the more responsive it becomes, like a muscle. It's actually even more responsive than a muscle. You use your chi during yoga, Reiki, acupuncture, tai chi and martial arts. It's a great practice, while using your chi, to have an intention in your mind and heart of an unwanted thought or energy and let it release. Also to hold the intention in your mind and heart of a positive thought and energy that serves you in your life. This is a powerful tool to support health, wellness and prosperity in your life.

7. Mantra Meditation 5-7+ years

Mantra "that which protects the mind" and "to free the mind." Mantra Meditations are words, sounds or phrases that are repeated out loud or said internally. Mantra Meditation dates back before Buddha. Words are prayers and they have sacred powers. Use words that are positive and that have a good intention. Because when you speak them, the words you say often come true.

Activity:

There are a few steps for Mantra Meditation
Find your Mantra word or phrase "to free the mind."

For example: I am peaceful…
Repeat the Mantra several times you can use prayer beads to assist you. Moving through each bead one at a time, repeat the mantra with each bead. Take a deep relaxing breath as you move through the mantra.

You can move through the beads with the tips of your middle finger and thumb. Move through half of the beads with one hand, then use the other hand and move through the rest of the beads. When you are practicing Mantra meditation, it's often helpful to listen to some relaxing music. This helps you focus your attention on your practice of Mantra Meditation.

Key Points:

- Combining sound, breath and rhythmic repetition
- Moves positive energy through the mind and body channels
- Regulates both sides of the brain
- Balances the nervous system
- Reduces stress and tension
- Balances the endocrine system, balances mood and overall well being
- Enhances compassion
- Boost the immune system

8. Music Meditation - 0+ years

Music can be used in conjunction with most meditations to help the mind relax. It can help deepen the relaxation and enhance the meditation.

Music Meditation can be used to help you to fall asleep, study, write in a journal or just relax.

Activity:

Look online or visit the local library and listen to meditation music. There are even apps that have meditation music. Listen and enjoy. You can use this time to write, practice yoga or study.

What else do you enjoy while listening to music meditation?

Key Point:

- Deepens the meditation - especially for beginners

9. Visualization Meditation

This is one of the most creative ways to meditate. Visualization uses the imagination to move through different locations and conditions to create a perfect environment. The mind concentrates while the body relaxes.

As much as your imagination will allow you, you can see and hear pleasant things. For example, sitting on a mountaintop and feeling the wind on your cheeks. You can visualize images and ideas to engage your mind.

Activity:

Read aloud

If it is safe to do so, close your eyes or focus your gaze on a small area. Start by relaxing your muscles. When thoughts come to mind, allow them to leave as easily as they came… thinking "Hmmm" or "Oh well" and turn your attention back to your body.

Let your muscles become loose and relaxed, starting with your feet… your ankles…. lower legs…. knees…. upper legs…. pelvis…. torso… back…. shoulders…. arms…. hands…. face…. and head.

Feel your body…. loose and relaxed.
Turn your attention now to your breathing. Without trying to change your breathing in any way, notice each breath…. just observe…. As thoughts arise, acknowledge them and let them go, returning your attention to your breathing….
Breathe naturally…. slowly…. As your thoughts wander, simply return your attention to your breathing.
Notice your breath as it flows gently in and out of your body…. without any effort….

Let's begin…

Imagine you're walking down a quiet lane. The weather is perfect and you're enjoying the steady rhythm of your footsteps as you move along at an easy, comfortable pace. It must have rained here recently, because the air is especially crisp and clear…., you can smell the fresh fragrance of flowers on the gentle breeze. As you're walking down the quiet lane, you notice some footprints, just ahead of you… alongside of you… and behind you.

There are tall oak trees along this lane and you're enjoying their shade and the soft rustle of their fallen leaves. You begin to follow the footprints. As if they are guiding you to right under one of the old oak trees. You make a comfortable place to sit, where you can lean against the trunk. Before you move on with your journey, you carefully move away some fallen leaves and make your comfy spot to rest. The earth is warm; the breeze is cool on your skin. As you rest your back on the sturdy and strong trunk, feel the warmth of your beating heart. Its beat is as strong as the old oak tree is strong.

Place your hands in prayer position over your heart. Now feel your beating heart, calming you. Feel the rhythm. Enjoy the quiet moment of your heart thumping. This rhythm pulls off any residue that needs to leave you, softens your breath, strengthens and relaxes you.

You are fully supported by the earth and the strong oak tree. Take a deep breath. Count backwards for 5, 4, 3, 2, 1 …. release.

You are remembering now the footprints that led you to this loving place that you hold deeply in your heart. You know that you have been guided here to center and relax. While sitting under the oak tree, know the earth holds you up, not your body.

You are just as sound and solid as the rocks are, under the ground that supports you.

Relax here under the old oak tree for a quiet rest….

Take a deep belly breath and beginning to slowly open your eyes! Your smile and heart are bursting full! Ahhhh! Your eyes begin to flutter open. Now take a nice long stretch and gently move your body around. Being present in the now moment, begin again on your peaceful walk, one step at a time.

Key points:

- Expands creativity
- Uses the mind to influence the body
- Reduces stress

- Boost immunity
- Relieves insomnia
- Alleviates headaches and chronic pain

10. Art Meditation: 2+ years

Art meditation is gazing at visually pleasing artistic pieces or images. It can encourage different thoughts. During the journey of meditation, art meditation offers moments of reflection. Adding affirmations (positive words) and meditation quotes to the art adds a powerful combination of visually pleasing and positive thoughts.

Activity:

Find or draw a picture of a beautiful image or visit a beautiful location. Example a museum, the ocean or a mountain. Or paint /color a picture with your favorite colors.
Add your Mantra and or affirmation.

Affirmation: Words or phrases to affirm.

Key Points:

- Relaxing
- Peace of mind
- Positive conditioning of the mind

Mya

People and Personalities

There are many people in the world and many types of personalities. These personalities are what make us unique. Everyone you know comes with his or her own personality that can even influence and affect your life. Your personality can influence and affect others lives, as well. Let's explore four types of personalities or "character" types. In these character types you may recognize someone you know, or even yourself!

- Cheerleaders – are people who bring out the best in you and a situation. The cheerleaders know that being their best is the key to working and living well.
- Advocates – are people who are enthusiastic and charismatic leaders. The advocates are passionate about their values in which

they believe. The advocates strive to accomplish goals and do what is right.

- Energy Shifters- if you have a low energy field, energy vampires can try to drain the energy out of you. The energy shifters are the "victims." They are highly suggestive, moody and gloomy people. They shift, happy positive energy, to gloomy negative, energy. Misery loves company. They look to negatively influence you. In other words, they look to make you miserable, too.

- Drama Kings and Queens – These people are demanding and overbearing. They love all the attention and want to be in the spotlight at all times. The drama kings and queens overreact in minor situations that can be easily being solved. Likewise, they shut down in a major situation that needs time and care.

Cheerleader

Drama Queen

Energy Shifter

Do you recognize any of these "character" types in people that you know?

Are you one of the four types of personalities described above?

Can you think of other personality types?

Perhaps you know how it feels to be surround by the "cheerleader" or the "advocate." These are people that can make you feel good, safe and inspired.

Perhaps you also know how it feels to be surround by people that make you feel uncomfortable and uneasy…an Energy Shifter or a Drama King or Queen. Those that ask you to dim your light in their presence?

Maybe you can think of some of these personalities right now. No judgment placed on anyone's character, just noticing the different types of characters.

Here are some tips on what to do when you're around those characters that make you feel a bit uneasy or uncomfortable.

The tips are…stand firmly on the ground, take a few deep breaths and center. Send energy and positive attention to the places that need it the most:

Stomach - your power center
Heart - your compassion center
Throat - your communication center
Head - you intellectual center

Notice where you are, what you are doing and how you are standing. Stand firmly on the ground. Are you holding a phone? Are you sitting or standing? Notice the now moment. Take your power in this moment and always.

Keeping your power is a tip that goes a long way. It is easy to do, and helps you gain focus and balance.

A Mantra for Protection

Mantra for protection from people that may send out a negative energy to you, regardless if they intend to or not:

Repeat 10 or more times out loud twice a day. When you wake every morning and when you go to sleep every night .

"All day, every day, in every way, I am getting better." Also " Nothing from without can touch the perfect light within me, I am always guided and protected."

Note –

Be glad it's not you that is creating the negative energy.
If you are creating the negative energy, why?
What are some steps you can do to turn your frown upside down?
Smile and send out your best.
Move away from them.
Learn not to be the annoyer.
Dealing with the annoyances builds emotional muscles, just like lifting weights in the gym builds body muscle.

Acceptance is Key To the Door of Success

Gratitude is possibly the single most important relationship we can create with the Universe. It's the bridge between where we are now and where we want to be in our near future. In the middle of a confusion, looking for something to be grateful for automatically uplifts us. It's impossible to be in the vibration of pessimism or a bad attitude and gratitude at the same time.

Gratitude along with the acceptance of the situation at hand, shifts our perspective from being mired in negativity to searching for the positive. Be conscious of your breathing, continuing to dream, grow, believe and inspire. Always remember you are not alone. Reach out to a friend, teacher, parent, guardian, or elder to help uplift you to place of gratitude and acceptance in your life. Don't be to shy or to afraid to ask for guidance, some day they may need the same support from you.

This section is dedicated to exploring different types of meditations, mantras, personality types and "co-creating" with others in the exploration.

Now that the pathway is opening for continuing these practices in your life and the pathway is lit with your shining light from within, let's add flowers along the pathway…bright beautiful flowers of…acceptance!

This is a pathway of self- discovery. It will help expand your mind, control your thoughts, cultivate your creative process and warm your heart. As this pathway opens wider, allow yourself to fully accept what is occurring in your life at any given moment. Then allow the moment to pass, giving way to a new moment close at hand. Letting the moment pass helps you stay in control of the new moment at hand.

Acceptance is the key to being able to move past what is going on now, into what to will be happening next. Without an acceptance, you can often stay in a place and never move past it. Be brave to sing a new song, a song of moving along. Read new books, start a new hobby. Be a teacher and a student of life. Be guided by your own inner compass to the new positive moments in your life!

Activity: Attitude of Gratitude

Name or draw a person, place or thing that you are grateful for.

Ex. Food, family time

"Ease on down
Ease on down the road
Ease on down

Ease on down the road
Don't you carry nothing that might be a load
Come on, ease on down
Ease on down the road"

Chorus from "Ease On Down the Road" from - *The Wiz*
The 1978 musical from Universal Pictures and Motown Productions; featuring Dina Ross and Michael Jackson.

Perhaps there are precious moments and people in your life that continue to move along the pathway of life with you. These people are mostly likely your close family and friends. This is a strong example of acceptance. To continue to stay in each other's lives, come what may, is one of the strongest examples of acceptance. It creates even more precious moments of happy memories, happy people and happy thoughts of the future. This keeps your energy vibration high; soaring like a kite!

What are some of your interest? Perhaps you have a new interest or perhaps you are just contemplating and exploring some new interest. For example it could be a new book, hobby, class, sport or martial arts practice?

_____

Is there something new in your life that you accept? Is there something in you life that you want to try to begin to accept? For example, a new responsibility, class or job?

_____

Is there something that has happened that you are still working on accepting? For example, a challenge or change in your life?

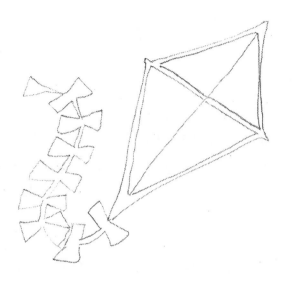

Kite Effect

Compare yourself to a kite. A kite needs two things to stay high in the sky : the wind to keep it afloat (your high energy) and the anchor to keep it from flying away. The anchor is your grounding acceptance. The wind and the anchor work together to keep the kite high in the sky. The same type of thing occurs when your high energy and grounding acceptance work together to keep you afloat in the sky of life. Seeing above you, below you and around you makes it easier when new things come into your life. Why? With this eagle eyesight, you most likely will already see something coming and you will be prepared…. this is the kite effect.

Acceptance is not allowing negative things to continue to happen in your life. The concept is the opposite of what the word might imply. Acceptance in this sense means when you are aware of where you are, then you know where you are going.

Be Prepared

Imagine that you have been looking forward to going on a big vacation. And you are going, now! What do you need to do before you leave? Most likely you will need to take care of a few things like cleaning your room, washing the dishes, and taking out the trash.

Cleaning up before you leave is important. Then, when you return home, your room will be clean. No dirt or dust will grow while you are away. You also pack what you need to bring with you, maybe saving room in your suitcase for some great gifts you will find on your travels.

Getting prepared for a big trip is like getting prepared for the acceptance of where you are in your life. It's like taking out the "internal" trash, washing and cleaning your energy, dusting off your heart and saving some space for more ideas and lessons that you will learn along the pathway of your life. Leaving things a mess and undone, can start a trend. Therefore a mess and things left undone can be what you're accepting in your life. Wow! Did you ever think of things this way?

However if you can have the sight to see, to clear all this dirt and dust away, you have made it past the challenge! You have accepted what you need, whether you see it good or bad. You have moved on. The next step while things remain squeaky clean is to focus now on the most important activity of all! You!

Focus Wheel

Bring to your attention to the things that really matter to you. Focus on what you would like to see happen in a situation in your life. It's very important not to focus on what you don't want to happen in your life, think positive thoughts in your day. This will bring positive actions in your day.

A focus wheel diagram helps you bring your positive attention to where it needs to be, in the present moment. It also tells you where you want to go next. What is important to you? What is it that would make you happy and that can become a reality? Something that can happen, once you put your positive attention and focus on it. In other words, an attainable goal!

By creating a focus wheel, you are setting positive emotional goals and allowing these goal's emotions to become a part of you. You will realize that you can actually have what it is you have been wanting.

Focus Wheel Activity

Let's use getting a good grade on an upcoming test, as an example of a "goal." What are some key words, images or colors that can help you reach your goal?

Directions: There is one middle circle and seven outer circles. The middle circle is your "goal." The other seven circles are steps to help you reach your "goal."

Fill in some of the outer circles with affirmative words. Declare these words.

Word Examples: "I remember my work" "This test is a challenge that I can meet " "I understand the material" "I have a study partner" "I feel excited about getting an "A" "I am smart" "I am a great student" "I am focused" "I will be calm during my test" " I am prepared."

Colors: The color blue is calming and relaxing. It is also associated with the act of communication. During your test you will be communicating with yourself that you know and understand your material. This can result in a great grade. The colors red and green are proven to help with concentration.

Image: A+ image, graduation cap, thumbs up.

Use an existing image or draw one.

Note: Different colors are associated with different emotions and attributes. See the Reiki Energy Chapter, under the Chakra section to learn more. Also, you can research color therapy at your local library or online.

See the focus wheel diagram on the next page.
1. Place your "goal" in the middle circle of your focus wheel.

Example: Get a good grade on my test.

2. Fill in the first outer circles (to the left of the center circle, going clockwise) with a word, color, or image.

3. Repeat this process filling in all the outer rings going clockwise.

4. Study your focus wheel. Is there a word, color, or image with which you are not comfortable? If so, remove it and find another word, color, or image that you feel comfortable to help you reach your goal.

5. Place your wheel where you want and continue to study it while preparing for your test.

Infinite Focus Wheel

Creating more focus wheels for a second, third, and fourth goal that would relate to the first goal and logically come next.

Infinite Focus Wheel Activity:

Example : Building your education and work resume

First goal - Good Grades

Second goal – Honor Roll

Third goal - Scholarship / Interview

Fourth goal – College / Job

Build on your first Focus Wheel and create more to enhance your long - term goal.

The Focus Wheel Process was presented by
-Abraham Hicks

"How do you feel about those things that you are giving most of your attention to? If there is something in your life that gives you negative emotion almost every time you think about it, we would do anything that we could do to get that negative thing out of our awareness." ~ Abraham-Hicks

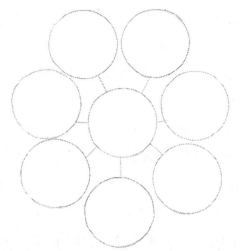

The Mind Body Awareness Experience, Continuing to Cross Training ™

There is so much knowledge and power that you have learned through the journey of reading and working through the all of the actives, meditations and more in Creating a Space for a Youth to Meditate.

Cross training – training in two or more activities in order to improve performance in a main practice.

The Mind Body Awareness Experience- the cross training of eastern practices, such as meditation, yoga, mantras, mudras, energy practices such as Reiki and Qigong. Also included are martial arts, healthy diet, mindfulness, respect, the discipline and devotion to make these practices a part of your daily life…for a lifetime.

By continuing the practices in Creating a Space for a Youth to Meditate, as part of your life, you are on your way to being committed to the Mind Body Awareness Experience (MBAE). The seed has been planted and it will continue to grow each time you devote yourself to your personal practice. Until the Mind Body Awareness Experience, becomes a habit, it may be hard to remember the feeling and personal space that (MBAE) brings. If it's hard to remember and hard to find time, life's positive and negative situations may urge you to recall the feeling these practices (MBAE) bring. You can always come back to these practices to create your experience again and again…. and above all share your experiences with others.

Infinity means to never end, continuous.

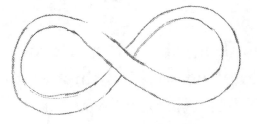

Yoga and You

Chapter notes for Guide / Support person

Use of yoga for Health in the United States

According to the 2007 National Health Interview Survey (NHIS), which included a comprehensive survey of complementary health used by Americans, yoga is the sixth most commonly used complementary practice among adults. More than 13 million adults practiced yoga in the previous year. Between 2002 and 2007 NHIS's use of yoga among adults increased by one percent or approximately three million people. The 2007 survey also found that more than 1.5 million children practiced yoga in the previous year.

The 2012 study indicates that 8.7 percent of U.S. adults, or 20.4 million people, practice yoga. Of current non-practitioners, 44.4 percent of Americans call themselves "aspirational yogis"—people who are interested in trying yoga.

-Yoga Journal

Many people who practice yoga do so to maintain their health and well being, improve physical fitness, relieve stress and enhance the quality of life. In addition, yoga is also used to address specific health conditions, such as back pain, neck pain, arthritis and anxiety. When practiced appropriately under the guidance of a well-trained instructor, yoga is generally low-impact and safe for healthy people.

As suggested by the National Center of Complementary and Alternative Medicine (NCCAM):

Practice safely and mindfully. Everyone's body is different and yoga postures should be modified based on individual abilities. Carefully select an instructor who is experienced and is attentive to your needs. This is an important step toward helping you practice yoga safely. Inform your instructor about any medical issues you have and ask about the physical demands of yoga.

Talk to your health care providers about any complementary health practices you use including yoga. If you are thinking about practicing yoga, also be sure to talk to your health care providers. Give them a full picture of what you need to do to manage your health. This will ensure coordinated and safe care.

Yoga and You is a "go to guide" with tips and techniques for anyone that has a youth in their life. The "go to guide" covers topics highlighting the benefits, types of yoga, poses, activities and ideas. Yoga and You is for those who are familiar with yoga and want to learn more, or are new to yoga and are ready to explore the ancient practice with a modern twist.

Q & A with Rhonda Jones

Author of Detox your Life and Awaken your Inner Spirit

Rhonda Jones received her 200-hour yoga certification, RYT at the Niroga Center in Berkeley, CA. Her classes incorporate various yoga disciplines including Raja, Vinyasa flow, and meditation. Rhonda has practiced yoga for the last 3 years and offers a variety of yoga classes for strength, flexibility, relaxation and mindfulness.

Rhonda Jones is the creator of over 25 meditation and affirmation CD's and is the author of a 10-week makeover program, Detox Your Life and Awaken Your Inner Spirit. To learn more visit www. detoxyourlifenow.com

A combination of profound collections including original meditations, affirmations, programs, yoga classes, retreats and more, are the powerful offerings Rhonda Jones contributes to her clients. These powerful offerings of a healthy and stress free life for adults show up as positive reflections to the youth.

Q- How has meditation helped your life?

A- Meditation helped me overcome years of depression. Meditation helped me slow down and begin to observe my mind and destructive thinking. Once I was aware of the voices in my head I was able to delete them. I believe meditation is like a shower of the mind. Each time we enter into that quiet space, it purifies our heart and mind. Ongoing and consistent meditation promotes peace of mind and inner awareness.

Q- How long have you been meditating?

A- I was first introduced to meditation during my first year in college. However, I did not maintain a consistent practice with knowledge and purpose. After realizing the value of meditation, it has been a regular practice in my life for the past 7 years.

Q- Why do you recommend this practice to people?

A- I believe all people suffer from the mental illness of thinking. This wouldn't be a problem except that most people's minds are filled with negativity and they don't even realize it. Then our unconscious thoughts direct our life and our habits. Most of us are a slave to our thoughts. Meditation, silence, and solitude help us to break the cycle of unconscious living and thinking.

Q- Tell me about your meditation retreats?

A-The last several years I have sponsored the Be Still, Meditation and Yoga Retreat. The retreat lasts 4 days and 3 nights and includes guided meditation instruction and yoga.

Q -What types of meditation do you practice / or teach?

A - I practice and teach a variety of meditation techniques that include guided meditation, mantra meditation, and centering prayer.

Q -How do you teach and to whom?

A - On my website, there are a variety of meditation CD's and downloads. I also provide several online courses, video tutorials, books, e-books, and other meditation resources. In addition to the website, I teach local classes and workshops periodically as well as hosting retreats.

Q- How often do you meditate?

A- My goal is to meditate once per day for 20-30 minutes. On average I probably meditate 3-5 times per week. Usually I meditate first thing in the morning. I believe that people should meditate at 20 minutes per session in order to get the greatest benefit as it takes a while for the mind to calm down.

Q- How do you describe meditation?

A- Meditation is like a shower of the mind.

Q- How do you feel that meditation can help children now and into their adult lives?

A- As children grow up they are bombarded with constant messages from their family, their teachers, their friends, the media, their environment, and more. These messages, whether good or bad, begin to attach themselves and are often internalized. As the layers and layers deepen, they begin to forget who they really are. They become what the outside world has conditioned them to be. They lose their internal compass as well as their creativity. They forget that they are divine beings that were created for greatness and purpose. Instead of pursuing their potential, they live distracted lives filled with the pursuit of material gain and pleasure.

I believe meditation practice started at a young age can help children connect to their inner spirit and awaken the sleeping giant within them. By learning to detach themselves from worldly enticements, distractions, and lies, children can realize the good that lives within them and follow a path of true light, awakening and true fulfillment.

----End chapter notes---

Types of yoga styles covered in this chapter:

- ❖ Ananda Yoga
- ❖ Anusara Yoga
- ❖ Bikram Yoga
- ❖ Integral Yoga
- ❖ Iyengar Yoga
- ❖ Kali Ray Triyoga
- ❖ Kripalu Yoga
- ❖ Kundalini Yoga
- ❖ Sivananda Yoga
- ❖ Svaroopa Yoga

Within these different styles, there are many benefits of yoga for today's youth. This chapter covers eight of these benefits. They are listed below and will be highlighted later in the chapter:

- Enhances Concentration
- Increases Self- Esteem
- Cultivates a Relaxed and Peaceful State of Mind and Body
- Maintains Strength and Flexibility in Growing Bodies
- Teaches Present Moment Awareness / "The Power of Now"
- Sparks Creativity and Ripens Imagination
- Encourages Kind Peer and Social Interactions
- Teaches Responsibility and Discipline

History

Yoga has been around for thousands of years. It is a long lasting ancient art. Yoga means "binding" or "union," because it binds your mind, body and heart into the exercise. The idea is to think about the pose and how to create a body- flow for your mind. This creates the mind body connection. Then a pose can be created and gracefully held for the duration.

For thousands of years many have loved 'binding" the beats to the rhythm of the music of the mind and the body. This unity of mind and body is the common practice in yoga. Yoga is a term, commonly know for physical, mental and spiritual practices or disciplines that originated in ancient India. Yoga's purpose is to attain a state of permanent peace and self- enlightenment.

By the turn of the first millennium, Hatha Yoga emerged as prominent tradition. Hatha Yoga is the style that many people associate with the word of yoga today. Hatha Yoga describes any of the physical practices of yoga. One of the Hatha Yoga traditions is Asana. Asana is the art and mastery of sitting poses "to sit down" and "sitting still." Asana, in modern times can be defined, not only as a sitting pose, but also as a physical yoga posture. Yoga is an exercise. This exercise is a great way to strengthen the body's core, while at the same time helping to control the thoughts in the mind.

Why is enjoying exercise fun and good for you? Because when you move around it starts your heart pumping and your blood begins to flow, your cheeks get warm and you feel strong and mighty! Yoga is a great way to exercise, strengthen your core and control your mind. As you move from one pose to another pose, yoga also strengthens your muscles and it helps you focus. Yoga also will help you become self-assured, focused, and responsible to yourself and the world. For example, you know how you may be looking for something and it's been right in front of you the whole time? Well, this ancient art can help you focus and find what it is you are looking for faster!

Eight Benefits of Yoga for Youth:

1. Enhances Concentration:

A young mind is like a sponge and can retain a lot of information. Hand / eye coordination and focus are important parts of high levels of learning and memory. Yoga engages both hand /eye coordination, moving into poses and then focusing to hold the poses. Focus holding the poses, while holding concentration on motion and stillness. Yoga allows the young mind to remain open and continue to expand.

2. Increases Self Esteem:

Although yoga movements are usually slow, to be practiced correctly, attention and focus is necessary. Endorphins (chemicals in the body that create a feeling of well being, comfort and relaxation) are increasing. When the endorphins are increasing, a happy feeling is created.

At the same time, toxins (a chemicals in the body that can have harmful effects) are being released and the body becomes relaxed. This creates a great feeling in the mind and body, as well. The increase of the endorphins and the decrease of the toxins will naturally cultivate a positive feeling and extend self-esteem. Actually, this can help with anger management.

Note: Drinking water is always good during exercise!

3. Cultivates a Relaxed and Peaceful State of Mind and Body:

The yoga studio is quiet and the only sound is the teacher talking. There may be some soft music playing. This creates a "quiet time."

Many yoga poses are designed for detoxing the organs by deep breathing. This causes the body and mind to feel a high sensation of health and vitality; creating a peace in the mind, body and increased energy of the individual.

4. Maintains Strength and Flexibility in Growing Bodies:

Holding a posture for thirty seconds, or so, increases physical strength. Likewise, holding your body in one position and stretching your muscles to achieve the poses on which you are focusing, requires strength and flexibility of the body and mind. This gradually increases your strength in that area of your body. In other words strength is developed without stressing the body.

5. Teaches Present Moment Awareness "The Power of Now:"

Yoga does not allow for daydreaming or thinking of anything else other than what your body needs to be doing at that very moment! Actually, if concentration is absent, you will most likely wobble and fall out of the pose. Then refocusing your attention to move back into the pose requires you to restore the "power of now."

Focusing on the "now" moment is a must while practicing yoga and achieving stability in the movement. When you are too focused on yesterday or tomorrow, what's happening right now is missed. This is a lesson to be carried on throughout life.

6. Sparks Creativity and Ripens Imagination:

Most kid's yoga classes have themes that are fun and engaging. The theme "Jungle Safari," comes to mind. Youth are given an opportunity to make up their own yoga poses according to the theme. The idea is to be inspired to use their imagination and share it with others. This is a time for them to be free and creative, thus creating self-expression.

7. Encourages Kind Peer and Social Interactions:

Yoga teaches youth that all humanity is the same. No matter race, gender or belief, humanity is the same. We all have minds that create, hearts that love and voices that can speak the truth. Partner yoga teaches kids important social skills, patience and grace, that can last a lifetime.

8. Teaches Responsibility and Discipline:

Yoga is not always an instant gratifier, nor is it always easily mastered. It takes time, patience and practice. This discipline ripples out into the world of the youth and is reflected in relationships and responsibilities. This creates a better work ethic, self - reliance and ability to maintain commitments.

Yoga poses are named after animals, nature and the sun. You recreate these poses with your body. For example the Tree Pose.

Samara

Yoga is a powerful tool to help with school success. It can also be instrumental in helping you becoming a good friend, son or daughter. As a bonus, learning to take care of the body, organs and heart is a practice that will continue throughout your lifetime. Whatever is desired can usually be attained. To say the least, the success rate will be gratifying!

Q & A

If you have already practiced yoga, how has it been a powerful tool for you?

If you have not yet practiced yoga, how do you think it can help you focus in school?

How do you think the practice of yoga or the practice of listening can help you to be a better friend, son or daughter?

How do you feel after a yoga practice, playing games or sports?

How do you carry this feeling with you for the rest of the day?

Styles of Yoga

Ananda Yoga:
Developed by: Swami Yogananda

Ananda Yoga, is the classic style of yoga. This style works with controlling the subtle energies within you, especially the Chakras. Its objective is to use the energies to harmonize body, mind and emotions, and above all, awareness of the body and its energies. One unique part of Ananda Yoga is the use of silent affirmations during the practice. It is a way to directly and consciously unify the energies of the body, mind and emotions. Ananda is an inward and gentler form of exercise. It's not an athletic or aerobic practice.

Anusara Yoga:
Pronounced (a- nu-SAR-a)
Developed by: John Friend

Means to follow your heart
Anusara Yoga is a new form of yoga. It is described as heart oriented and spiritually inspiring. Participants have a deeper knowledge of the outer and inner body. However, all are welcome to practice.

Ashtanga Yoga / AKA Power Yoga:
Developed by: K. Pattabhi Jois

If you are looking for a serious workout this is the yoga style for you! Ashtanga is physically demanding. Moving from one posture to another, it builds flexibility, strength and stamina.

Bikram Yoga:
Founder: Bikram Choudhury studied yoga with Bishnua Ghosh, brother of Paramahansa Yogananda.

Bikram is HOT HOT HOT and you sweat, sweat, and sweat! The room is about 97 degrees and Bikram Yoga is "scientifically" designed to warm and to stretch muscles, ligaments and tendons.

Integral Yoga:
Developed by Swami Satchidananda.

Swami is the Yogi (a yoga practitioner) who introduces the chant "OM" to many. Integral Yoga's focus is on meditation and has been used to reverse heart disease.

Iyengar Yoga:
Developed by B.K.S. Iyengar

It's hard to appreciate how involved a simple thing like standing is. It's a matter of keeping your body on top of your legs. If you are standing with your arms to the sky, you are doing Tadasana, mountain pose. This can take some coordination and concentration.

B.K.S. Iyengar is one of the best-known Yogi's and the creator of this popular yoga style. Iyengar Yoga, is noted for its style and great attention to detail and precise alignment of postures. And the use of yoga belts and blocks can be used to assist you in the postures.

Kali Ray TriYoga:
Founded by Kali Ray

This style of yoga combines breath and posture together to create dynamic and intuitive flows. It combines flowing and sustained postures that are synchronized with breath and mudra.

Kripalu Yoga:
Named after Swami Kripalvananda

Often called the yoga of consciousness, Kripalu Yoga puts a great emphasis on alignment, coordinating breath, movement and proper breathing. This "honors the wisdom of the body." There are three stages in Kripalu Yoga. Stage One focuses on learning the postures for an extended time, and exploring your body's abilities. Stage Two involves holding the postures for an extended time, developing concentration and inner awareness. Stage Three is like a meditation in motion. The movements from one pose to another, fluidly arise unconsciously and spontaneously.

Kundalini Yoga:
In the tradition of Yogi Bhajan

Kundalini Yoga, focuses on the controlled releases of Kundalini energy. Classic poses, coordination of breath and movement meditation are involved.

Sivananda Yoga:
Founded by Swami Sivananda, one of the most influential spiritual teachers of the 20th century.

Sivananda is one of the world's largest schools of yoga. It follows a set structure that includes classic asanas (sitting poses) relaxation and pranayama (breath work). Pranayama is a Sanskrit word meaning breath. This style of yoga has been most popular since the 1960's.

Svaroopa Yoga:
Developed by Rama Berch

Focuses on opening and movement of the spine and teaches significantly different ways of doing familiar poses. This yoga style is a consciousness-oriented yoga that also emphasizes the development of inner experience more than focusing on regular poses.

Roan

You can always find a style of yoga that you like and is comfortable for you!

In the history section, it was learned that "yoga is an art" that is "binding." And art often times needs a canvas. A yoga mat is the canvas and your feet and hands are binding on this canvas to support your body in the poses. There are also yoga blocks, belts and balls to help support you, as well.

Now that the many yoga styles have been introduced, let's practice some!

Let's start by creating the space.

Tips and the Art of Yoga:

1. Find a comfortable space

2. It's best to have an empty stomach
3. Find a time that works every day to start a healthy routine
4. Bare feet on a non-slip surface or a yoga mat
5. Lay out your mat and give yourself arms length to move around
6. Turn on some soft music or a guided meditation, if you like
7. Take a few deep breaths and begin
8. Remember while your body is still growing, it's OK not to hold a pose for too long
9. Hold the pose for as long as you can and then move into the next pose

Chole

Yoga Vocabulary

There are different names for the many types of yoga poses.

Asana – Sitting and laying
Ashtanga Vinyasa – Flow yoga
Hatha – Physical yoga
Savasana – Sitting or laying pose

What are some other yoga names for poses and positions?

Example: Vriksasana – Tree Pose

During yoga practice, it is important to remember:

1. Alignment of your body
2. Proper breathing
3. Coordination of breath and movement

Waking Up Your Joints Activity!

FINGERS

Let's wake up your fingers
Facing forward hold your right hand in front of your heart
Inhale

Now with your left hand gently take the little finger of your right hand and move the finger back and forth
Exhale
Let your little finger bend back to its normal position
Inhale
While continuing to inhale and exhale
Repeat the activity with your other fingers
Switch hands and move through your left hand

WRISTS

With you palms facing your heart, move your left and right wrist one way
Inhale
Then the other way
Exhale
Repeat 10 times
Continuing to inhale and exhale in between
Now shake your hands and wrists till they feel loose

KNEES

Facing forward slowly bend your right leg and begin to raise it up toward your chest
Inhale
Hold the bottom of your thigh with both hands
Lift your right leg so that your knee is straight
Exhale

Look straight ahead and line your knee to your head
Hold that pose for a moment
Rotate your knee gently left to right
Now switch legs

FEET

With your feet facing forward, raise your right leg
Inhale
Hold your balance and move your foot and ankle around in a circle, 10 times
Exhale
Repeat with your left foot

HIPS

Facing forward with your hands on your hips
Move your hips back and then forward again
Inhale
Do this 5 times
Exhale
Now move in circles 10 times
Continue to inhale and exhale

Yeah! Your joints are awake and now you can being!

How mindful is your body? Let's practice!

Yoga Pose Diagrams

Yoga

TREE

CAT

CAT.

BOAT

LION

BRIDGE

DORMOUSE

LOTUS

SLEEPY

Yoga

MOUNTAIN

DOG

DOG

MOON

SUN SALUTE

SUN SALUTE

WARRIOR 1

WARRIOR 2

WARRIOR 3

As you know, yoga is the art of binding. It is also the art of imitating animals and nature and more:

Activity:

What's your favorite animal?

_____

Move around as your favorite animal would move. Does this animal make a sound? If it does, what sound does it make? Now, move into your favorite animal pose. Visualize or describe what this animal looks like.

Example: Dog Pose

_____

Activity:

What's your favorite pose?

_____

Imitate your favorite pose. Does it move, grow or change. How?

Example: The Warrior Pose has three different poses

_____

Sun Salutations

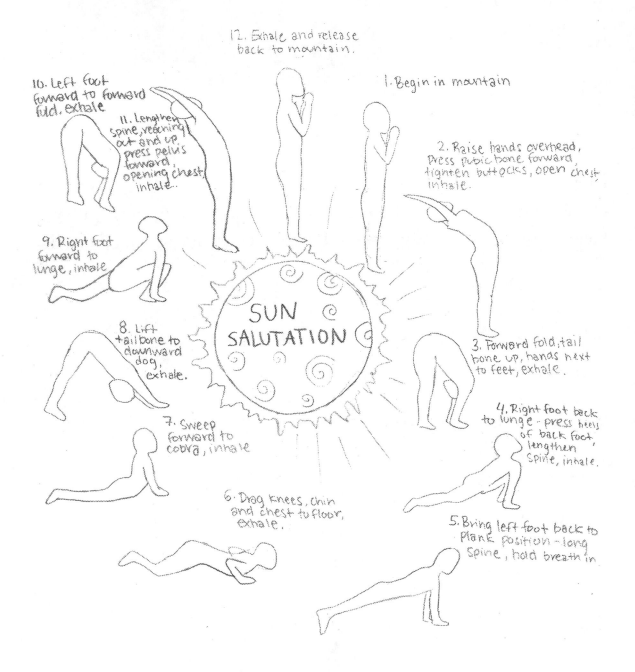

12. Exhale and release back to mountain.

1. Begin in mountain

2. Raise hands overhead, Press pubic bone forward, tighten buttocks, open chest, inhale.

10. Left foot forward to forward fold, exhale

11. Lengthen spine, reaching out and up, press pelvis forward, opening chest, inhale.

9. Right foot forward to lunge, inhale

SUN SALUTATION

3. Forward fold, tail bone up, hands next to feet, exhale.

8. Lift tailbone to downward dog, exhale.

4. Right foot back to lunge - press heels of back foot, lengthen spine, inhale.

7. Sweep forward to cobra, inhale

6. Drag knees, chin and chest to floor, exhale.

5. Bring left foot back to Plank position - long spine, hold breath in

Tori B. Amos

Suggested Daily Practice

- Wake Up Your Joints Exercise
- Sun Salutations
- Conclude with a few of your favorite poses
- You can choose what pose reflects your mood

Some days you may feel like practicing the mighty Lion Pose, another day perhaps the still Tree Pose

Note: If you need to rest in between poses, try doing the Savasana or Sleep Pose. (Lay on your back)

Pose and Its Reflection

Downward Dog Rejuvenating stretch
Cows Face Deep stretch of hips, ankles, thighs, shoulders, armpits, chest, deltoids and triceps

Eagle Standing focus pose, balance on one foot at a time

Turtle advanced pose, deep long stretch

Lotus ultimate power yoga, sitting pose

Camel back bending pose opens the whole front of the body

Bird strengthening pose, lifting your body off the mat

Horse standing, balance, focus

Caterpillar to Butterfly similar to the cow face and horse poses

Frog intense hip opener

Mouse relaxing forward lay

Owl twisting, balance, posture

Shark / Dolphin similar to downward dog, relaxing, helps with headache, backache.

Seal deep compression and stimulation of the lower back and abdomen

Crab both hands and feet on the ground, belly and head face up, balance and strength

Tree balancing on one foot with arms up, balance and focus pose

Cobra common yoga backbend

Lion kneeling and opening mouth wide and sticking out tongue with a mighty roar stimulates the vocal cords and relieves jaw tension

Childs Pose common relaxing laying pose

Elias, Naomi, Roan & Charlotte

Choose Your Animal Activity

What is your favorite animal pose, now?

_____

Why?

_____

Color in this animal pose, on the yoga poses diagram.

_____

Describe this animal pose and its reflection.

_____

Now choose a different animal to describe and color.

_____

After thinking about it, what's your favorite animal now, all of them?

_____

It's so much fun to move around and make animal sounds, becoming big and small, stretching and bending.

Word Find Yoga and You

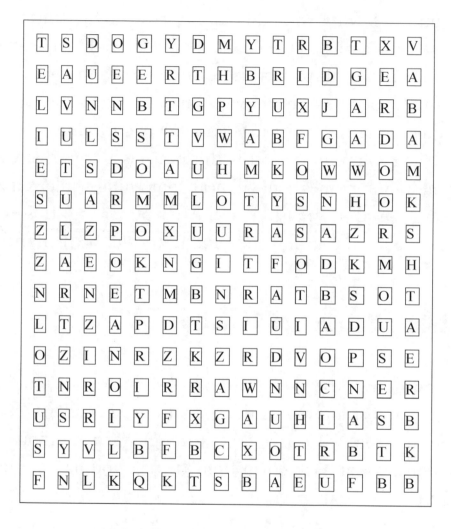

T	S	D	O	G	Y	D	M	Y	T	R	B	T	X	V
E	A	U	E	E	R	T	H	B	R	I	D	G	E	A
L	V	N	N	B	T	G	P	Y	U	X	J	A	R	B
I	U	L	S	S	T	V	W	A	B	F	G	A	D	A
E	T	S	D	O	A	U	H	M	K	O	W	W	O	M
S	U	A	R	M	M	L	O	T	Y	S	N	H	O	K
Z	L	Z	P	O	X	U	U	R	A	S	A	Z	R	S
Z	A	E	O	K	N	G	I	T	F	O	D	K	M	H
N	R	N	E	T	M	B	N	R	A	T	B	S	O	T
L	T	Z	A	P	D	T	S	I	U	I	A	D	U	A
O	Z	I	N	R	Z	K	Z	R	D	V	O	P	S	E
T	N	R	O	I	R	R	A	W	N	N	C	N	E	R
U	S	R	I	Y	F	X	G	A	U	H	I	A	S	B
S	Y	V	L	B	F	B	C	X	O	T	R	B	T	K
F	N	L	K	Q	K	T	S	B	A	E	U	F	B	B

ART	BINDING	BOAT
BREATH	BRIDGE	CANVAS
CAT	DOG	DOORMOUSE
LION	LOTUS	MOON
MOUNTAIN	SLEEP	SUNSALUTAIONS
TREE	WARRIOR	YOGA

Lotus is a Meditation and Concentration Pose

See your mind glowing white like a projector or the sunshine. Your mind is the projector of your heart. When your heart is calm and focused, your mind will project this calm focus. Can you be still and focus? Turn off your thoughts in your mind for just a moment. Is this hard? It's quiet time and it's up to you to quiet your mind. It's up to you to focus. When you want to be still, this peace is always there. You just have to find it. Sometimes you will hear something while you are still. If you hear a sound, try not to move. After practicing, this exercise it will get easier and your mind, body and heart will be thankful for it.

Focus While You Lotus Activity

Moving into Lotus Pose close your eyes, brighten your mind. Keep a good posture and straight back. Now continue "Focus As You Lotus." Start counting from 1-10. If you get through with no thoughts and/or distractions, count back down from 10-1. If you have a thought or become distracted, start over. Remember, getting from 1-10 without a distraction is a great job! If you are having a good time with "Focus While You Lotus" keep going for five minutes. Open your eyes slowly then move out of the pose.

Mya

Namaste

A custom after finishing with your yoga exercise is saying the word NAMASTE. Namaste means, "The spirit within me salutes the spirit within you." Placing your hands in front of your heart and bow to your instructor or yourself if you are alone. This gesture is acknowledging your heart energy and a deep form of respect to your instructor.

Science of the Heart and Mind

Did you know that your heart is more intelligent than your mind? For many years, it was thought that the brain did the communicating directly to the heart. Now research has shown that there is a two - way communication between the brain and the heart. It's an ongoing conversation. Each organ is continuously influencing each other's functions.

"The heart's electrical field is about 60 times greater in amplitude than the electrical activity generated by the brain. This field, measured in the form of an electrocardiogram (ECG), can be detected anywhere on the surface of the body. Furthermore, the magnetic field produced by the heart is more than 5,000 times greater in strength than the field generated by the brain and can be detected a number of feet away from the body, in all directions, using SQUID-based magnetometers."

Quoted from the Warrior Forum 2008 / Institute of HeartMath ®

Meditation Activities

Now, let's continue to explore different types of meditations and activities. It's important to keep in mind a "calm focus." You may revisit the practice you learned in the "Focus While You Lotus" a meditation activity. While you explore meditation, it is important to remember the heart and mind connection.

Mindful Walking Meditation

If you're too busy to sit and meditate during your day, try this!

Activity:

Look forward as you walk, with a straight back. Feel your steps and the ground holding you up. Concentrate on your breath and movement. Take the time to relax your brow, mind and shoulders. Focus more on getting to your destination safely, rather than on all the activities going on around you.

Warming Hands and Feet

Place your hands together
Rub them around in a circle

Feel them warming
Now place your hands over your eyes and face
Feel the warm vibration your moving energy creates
Bend your knees up and place your feet together
Rub them and warm them with your hands
Rock back and forth on your back
Raise your feet in the air
Cross your ankles and your arms
Hold your right calf with your left hand
Hold your left calf with your right hand
Move back and forth
Moving your weight from left to right
Moving your body to gently wake up

Sleep Time

"Time for bed," "Time to rest," "Time to dream."
Sometimes this may be easier said than done!
What to do when you are all snuggled under the covers and your eyes
are closed, but mind and body are still wide-awake.

Activity: Move and rock your body slowly. Motion can often times be
relaxing, like when driving in a car can make you sleepy, or like rocking
a baby gently to sleep.

Balloon Meditation / Visualization

Watch your worries disappear in a balloon!

Activity:

Fill up a balloon, what color is it?
You are filling the balloon with your worries. Know the balloon will float. When you're ready, set it free into the air. Look at the balloon as it floats away, floating higher and higher in the sky. Soon it will disappear.

Now take a deep breath and let it out.
How do you feel? Lighter?
If necessary, repeat this meditation and see if your worries stay away.

What color is the balloon? If it is a color of the rainbow, refer to the Reiki Energy Chapter. Do the Rainbow Meditation. Focus on the Chakra linked to the color of the balloon.

Hint – Red balloon,
Color - Red - Root Chakra

Seeing And Memory Activity

For this next activity, you will need a partner.
Place a few things in front of you.
Example:

Flower
Feather
Book
Toy
Shoe

Look at all of the objects.
Close your eyes while your partner removes one object. When you open your eyes, something is missing?

What is missing?

_____

Now it's your partner's turn to repeat the activity.

How mindful are you? When the activity is completed, how many objects did you notice were missing?

_____

Out of the four different meditations, Focus While You Lotus, Mindful Walking, Balloon and Sharing, which one(s) did you like the best?

_____

Which one(s) can you do without a distraction for five minutes or more?

_____

Wake Up Time Activity

"Time for school," "Time for practice," "Time to go!" These maybe some familiar words we hear when we wake in the morning. But before you even get out of the bed, here are a few "two-minute" wake up exercises for your body, mind and heart.

Note: You can have your yoga mat "canvas" right below your bed and you can roll onto it.

Stretching

Lay on your back raise your right hand up & point your left foot (opposite sides).
Take nice long breaths as you are stretching.
Make your body nice and long.
Lower your arm and leg.
Now do the same with the other leg and arm.

Sleep Time Mantra

Place your thumb on your pinky - I
Place your thumb on your ring finger - am
Place your thumb on your middle finger - peace
Place your thumb on your pointer finger - ful

I AM PEACEFUL

Note - Use both hands at the same time.

Repeat until you are sleep zzzzzzz

Devotion to your practice

Once your excitement about your yoga practice has been developed, if you choose, it can last a lifetime. Your yoga practice can be fulfilling and it can sustain you in many ways. Your mind will continue to be focused, your body will continue to be more flexible and your awareness will continue to grow.

The world is ever changing. People come and go in your life, your environment can change, the seasons change, the classes you study change. Also, there are many forms for yoga styles and yoga poses to learn and master along the way. Yet as long as your passion and your devotion for yoga remain, a yoga session is a time when all can stand still. You and the mat are all that remain, in the present moment. This is your safe steady place and space that you can control that will never change.

Reiki Energy

Chapter Notes for the Guide (support person)

This chapter is a "how to guide." It is an introduction to a powerful, yet gentle energy used for thousands of years. The energy is known as Reiki. This guide has details about the history of the Usui style of Reiki Energy. It includes the benefits of the attunement process, mindful activities and an explanation of energy fields such as Aura Layers and Chakras. Different meditations and games are included, as well.

Reiki for Children and Teens

The calming practice of Reiki promotes relaxation and confidence. Through Reiki, children and teens tap into "the Universal life energy" to defuse and unplug. Children and teens will enjoy their "me" time and hold onto its lasting effects. The gifts of Reiki, introduced at a young age, promotes a healthy way of living throughout adulthood. As children or teens grow throughout life, they will be more inclined to learn to make better choices and create balance.

Reiki Benefits for Children and Teens:

- Less likely to show signs of exaggerated excitability & depression
- Improves concentration, thus improving test scores
- Enhances relaxation and sleep
- Calms and promotes balance
- Enhances self-awareness and self-esteem
- Helps with asthma and many other illnesses

Reiki Benefits for Children and Teens

Reiki therapy is safe and non-invasive. It is used to facilitate relaxation and recovery, decrease anxiety and treats pain. Nursing homes, emergency rooms, operating rooms, organ transplant care units, pediatric, neonatal and OB/GYN units, often use Reiki to support their patients, too.

For example "Dr. Lawrence B. Palevsky, M.D., FAAP., received his medical degree from the NYU of Medicine in 1987. Dr. Palevsky is the President of the American Holistic Medical Association (AHMA) and President of the Holistic Pediatric Association. Palevsky integrates the use of western medicine and alternative therapies to treat children's illnesses."

"Dr. Palevsky incorporates Reiki into his treatments of various childhood ailments and experiences. His philosophy is healing the whole child, naturally. These include ADD/ ADHD, autism, asthma, eczema, allergies, inflammatory bowel disease, ear infections, learning disabilities, developmental delays, complex neurological conditions, side effects of chronic medication use, vaccination damage, respiratory infections, asthma and gastrointestinal upset. Also included are some ailments that once only plagued adults, such as Type 2 (adult-onset) diabetes."

"Along with a range of holistic practices, when treating these illnesses, Dr. Palevsky sees Reiki as a valuable part of care. Among this group of holistic practices are preventive medicine, nutrition, lifestyle changes, acupuncture and Chinese medicine, osteopathy, cranial- sacral therapy, environmental medicine, homeopathy, essential oils and natural healing modalities. Reiki also empowers children and teens with self-regulation and self-care."

Exerts from drpalevsky.com

ADD or ADHD

John M. Grohol, Psy. D., for Psych Central said in July of 2013, that there are recent steps in the understanding of ADHD:

1. It is estimated that up to 5 % of children in most cultures are affected -- approximately 3.5 million children in the US. In a classroom of 30 to 35 children, it is likely that at least two will have ADHD.

2. ADHD is among the most common mental disorders among children. It is one of the top reasons for referral to a pediatrician, family physician, a pediatric neurologist, child psychiatrist or psychologist. ADHD is best diagnosed by a child psychologist or other child specialist in ADHD.

3. ADHD is about three times more common among boys than girls.

4. The symptoms of ADHD do not always go away – up to 60 % of child patients retain their symptoms into adulthood.

5. ADHD has been identified in every nation and culture, in which it has been studied.

6. ADHD is often difficult for everyone involved. As well as the difficulty of living with the symptoms, others within the society also face challenges. Some experts have linked ADHD with an increased risk of accidents, drug abuse, and failure at school, antisocial behavior and criminal activity. But others view ADHD in a positive light, arguing that it is simply a different method of learning, which involves greater risk-taking and creativity.

Reiki can be very helpful with these issues. Of course, each situation is unique and a cure cannot be promised. However, for quite a long time, practitioners have been reporting positive results with behavior problems by using Reiki. Part of the key to this benefit regarding ADD or ADHD, is the flexibility that Reiki practitioners have regarding the application. Without touching or even being near the patient, the Reiki practitioner can simply be in the same room gently offering the energy.

Some practitioners just spend time with a small child, playing, coloring.... letting the child guide the action. As the child becomes more and more comfortable and as the energy begins to work, changes can be made in how Reik is received. An important factor in dealing with these issues is adjusting to the moment. Since Reiki works on all levels, mental and emotional as well as physical, the body will be able to use the energy to find a balance in its own way. As well as with many other natural healing techniques, changes using Reiki may come quickly or come gradually. So that the child can receive Reiki daily, it would be a wise choice for a parent to be trained in Reiki.

Excerpts from, Reiki Empowerment Group, (2004)

Autism

Reiki practitioners have also seen good results working with and training a child with Autism, Asperger's and other developmental syndromes. The causes of Autism are unknown and much controversy surrounds this disorder. Because Reiki is balancing, it can be of benefit, regardless of the cause. Reiki can provide soothing moments for parents and children and teens alike. Reiki helps them get rid of fear and worry. This naturally fosters more interest in positive things and behavior. As well as the benefits of empowerment, a child who learns Reiki also benefits from its centering effects.

-------image of the sun & key---

---end of chapter notes----

Meaning of Reiki

Pronounced : Ray – Key

(Rei- meaning 'spirit') Ki (meaning 'life force energy')

"Reiki is a Japanese technique of natural hands on healing and positive growth. Reiki always comes from the heart and a loving place. It's an energy that has a positive effect on all living things."

History of Usui Reiki & Dr. Mikao Usui

Dr. Mikao Usui was born in Japan. From birth, he was recognized as a special child. When Mikao Usui grew up, he became a doctor and unlocked many healing secrets. He also developed natural healing techniques. He taught several students his natural healing techniques and named these techniques Reiki. For the sake of humanity, Dr. Usui wanted to unravel the mysteries of the universe. In his studies, Usui learned Chinese and Sanskrit. He was then able to unlock and understand the ancient texts and sutras of different healing formulas.

During one of his classes, a student asked him if he believed that people could heal with their hands? At that time, Usui was not sure. Soon after that, Usui went to a Zen Monastery on the top of Mt. Kurama, located near Kyoto, Japan. He wondered about what his student had asked him and if it could be true. Can people really heal with their hands? Usui wanted to know the answer to this question!

Usui was at the Zen Monastery for twenty-one days. He put aside one stone a day, to mark twenty-one days of fasting and meditation. After day twenty-one he received a vision of light revealing to him the Reiki symbols and how to use them for healing through the hands. This was when Reiki Energy was re-discovered.

Because of Usui's devotion in learning the keys for deeper healing, today there are thousands of Reiki Masters and Reiki practitioners, all over the world, using Usui system of Reiki and their hands for healing.

It goes to show that if one has a question, ask it! If Usui's student had never asked him about healing with hands, Reiki might have remained silent for many more years.

Many believe that Mt. Kurama is the birthplace of the re-awaking of Reiki. Kurama is also the location of the annual Kurama Fire Festival that takes place every October. This area is now designated as a national treasure of Japan.

Reiki Attunement

A Reiki Attunement is a special hands on ceremony. In the ceremony, the Reiki Master places the Reiki energy and the Reiki symbols into the seven main Chakras of the body and into the Chakras of the hands, as well. After personally receiving a Reiki Level I attunement, Reiki can be independently practiced on yourself and on others. Even a child who has learned the techniques of Reiki can have great results giving Reiki to others.

Note : Chakra- Physical and energetic centers in the human body.

More Benefits of Reiki

Self-healing
Relieves pain

Helps sleep
Calming
Reduces stress
Improves attention and focus
Reiki never runs out or stops working

Activity:

Draw or list a person, animal or plant that you would like to experience positive energy or Reiki.

Creating an Energy Ball

Put your hands a few inches apart.
Now, without letting your hands touch, pull and push your hands apart, turning them around and around, like rolling a small ball.

Do you feel the energy ball forming in your hands?

What does it feel like?

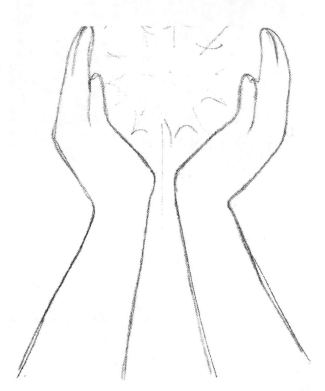

Every Living Being has Life Force Energy

This Life Force contains hundreds of Chakras and twelve Aura layers. Let's learn about the seven main Chakras and seven Aura layers.

Note: Aura – the distinctive atmosphere or quality that seems to surround and be generated by a person, thing or place.

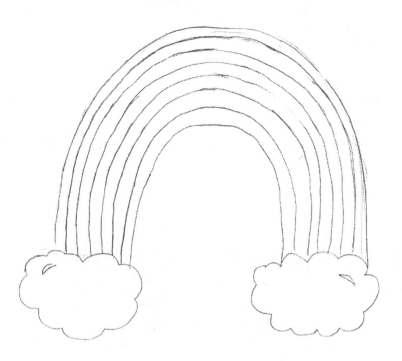

Seven Main Chakras

The Seven main Chakras are the colors of the rainbow

1st Chakra / Root
Color: Red

Represents your foundation and feelings of being grounded

Location: Base of spine in the tailbone area

Express: Survival, financial independence, money and food

2nd Chakra / Sacral
Color: Orange

Our connection and ability to accept others and new experiences

Location: Lower abdomen, about 1- 2 inches below the navel

Express: Creativity, relationships, pleasure

3rd Chakra / Solar Plexus
Color: Yellow

Our ability to be confident and in control of our lives

Location: Upper abdomen in the stomach area

Express: Sense of identity, self-worth, power center

4th Chakra / Heart
Color: Green

Our ability to love

Location: Center of the chest just above heart

Express: Love, joy, inner peace

5th Chakra / Throat
Color: Blue

Our ability to communicate

Location: Throat

Express: Communication, self–expression of feelings, the truth

6th Chakra / Brow Chakra
Color: Indigo

Our ability to focus and see the big picture

Location: Forehead between the eyes

Express: Intuition, imagination, wisdom, ability to think and make decisions

7th Chakra / Crown
Color: Violet

The highest Chakra represents your ability to be connected to higher consciousness

Location: The very top of the head

Express: Inner and outer beauty, our connection to a higher source

Tuning Chakra Activity

Say the vowel sound, hold the sound for five seconds.

1st Root Chakra : UH
2nd Sacral Chakra: OOO
3rd Solar Plexus: OH
4th Heart Chakra : AH
5th Throat Chakra : EYE
6th Brow Chakra : AYE
7th Crown Chakra: EEE

As you are saying the vowel sounds for five seconds each. Notice your feeling around the chakra you are tuning.

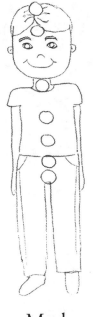

Marley

Aura

The aura energies surround the physical body and vibrate; so quickly that we can't see them. They are composed of tiny energy lines, like sparkling webs of light that are similar to the lines of a television screen. Image an "egg" like shape surrounding all living things. However, just because you may not see your aura, doesn't mean it's not there. Like, the feeling of happiness, comfort and love. All living beings have auras. These energy fields connect you to the rest of the world and allow you to exchange feelings and emotions with other living things.

Aura Layer Activity

While learning about the Aura layers, you will also be doing the Aura layer activity. After learning about each Aura layer, you will then color in the aura layer.

You will need:
A sheet of paper, markers or crayons: red, orange, yellow, green, blue, purple / indigo and violet

Directions:

On a separate piece of paper, in the center, draw a picture of yourself. You will color in seven Aura layers around the picture of yourself.

Color the Aura layer with the same color that it represents.

Hint: Aura colors are the colors of the rainbow. You will start with the first color of the rainbow, red.

The Seven Layers of the Aura Fields Activity

1st layer Aura layer / The Etheric Body
Pronounced - E-ther-ic
Color: Red
Location: Closest to your body

This is a blueprint of your physical body, made of energy and light. Nearest to your body is the Etheric Aura. This layer has to do with your bodies' physical growth; its strength and weakness. Physical feeling of satisfaction and dissatisfaction are also a part of influencing your Etheric Aura. If you are happy and enjoying life, this energy is very strong. The Etheric Body extends a quarter of an inch outside the skin of the physical body. Related to the First Chakra – Root.

- Draw a red egg shaped around the drawing of yourself.
- Label Etheric Body

What are some satisfying things that you experienced today?
What are some dissatisfying things that you experienced today?

2nd Layer / Emotional Body
Color: Orange

This layer is made up of your emotions and feelings. They are represented in the Emotional Aura. It expresses and reflects your mood at the present time. For example: anger, fear, grief, love, happiness and comfort. The Emotional Body extends three inches from the physical body. Related to the Second Chakra – Sacral.

- List an emotion (s)

_____

- Draw an orange egg like shape around the red line.
  Label Emotional Body

3rd Layer / Mental Body
Color: Yellow

This body contains your thoughts and belief system, containing everything you have ever learned. It is also associated with the vibrational level of the thoughts and the mental processes of the ego. The light of this layer will appear stronger when you are connecting to mental tasks. The Mental Body extends up three inches – eight inches around from the physical body. Related to the Third Chakra – Solar Plexus.

Name something new, or something that you would like to share that you have learned.

_____

- Draw a yellow egg like shape around the orange line.
- Label Mental Body

Note: Ego —A person's sense of self-esteem or self-importance

4th Layer/ Astral Body
Color: GREEN

This body contains your connection to your higher self, by connecting to yourself on an emotional and physical level. When you feel upbeat and positive, your aura is more full and thicker. When your emotions are heavy and sad, your aura is thinner. The Astral Body extends up to one-half foot up above and one foot around from the physical body. Related to the Fourth Chakra- Heart.

- Name something nice that you have done, that made you feel good in your higher self.

_____

Hint: Something that made you feel good, or something you did to help uplift someone else.

- Draw an egg like shape around the yellow line, green
- Label Astral Body

5th Layer/ The Etheric Template
Color: BLUE

You see and sense with your five senses in this body and it's made up of many different parts, like organs and bones. It is associated with aspects of the physical body and is known as a blueprint of the lower Etheric body, where matter is shaped into the physical aspect. The Etheric Template extends from one to two feet around the physical body, to one and one-half up to, two feet around from the physical body. Related to the Fifth Chakra – Throat.

List 3 organs:
1.
2.
3.

List 3 bones:
1.
2.
3.

- Draw a blue egg like shape around the green line.
- Label it Etheric Template

6th Layer / The Celestial Body
Color: INDIGO

This layer is exclusively composed of light and is know as the level of higher thought. It gives you access to higher qualities of feelings, thoughts and manifestations. This body brings your dreams and hopes into reality. The Celestial Body extends two feet, to three feet around the physical body. Related to the Sixth Chakra – Brow.

What is a dream of yours that you would like to see become reality?

Note: A wish, hope, desires or dream that comes true is one of the examples of manifestation.

- Draw a purple / indigo egg like shape around the blue line.
- Label it Celestial Body

7th Layer / Ketheric or Causal Body.
Color :VIOLET

This layer is connected to the universal and global consciousness. It is the closest connection, to a higher source and power. It extends two feet up and one-half foot around the physical body. Related to the Seventh Chakra – Crown.

- Draw a violet egg like shape around the purple / indigo line.
- Label it Ketheric or Causal Body

Visualize the Rainbow Mediation

Close your eyes. Deeply breathe in three times.

1st Red / Root Chakra

Feel the Red Bow filling up and across your hips and tailbone. Your roots are strong, deeply rooted into the earth. You are rooted and grounded. You are secure.

Affirmation: You know yourself and make choices you know to be right.

Send attention to your legs and bones

2nd Orange / Sacral Chakra

Feel the Orange Bow filling up and around your belly button. You are creative in your own expression.
You are understood in all of your relationships.

Affirmation: Honor your creativity and positive thoughts.

Send attention to your lower belly area.

3rd Yellow / Solar Plexus

Feel the Yellow Bow filling up your stomach.

You are confident within yourself. You are powerful within yourself.

You are an important part of your school and community.

Affirmation: You have a deep, healthy, even flow. Your feelings have value and you are important.

Send attention to your middle organs.

4th GREEN / Heart Chakra

Feel the Green Bow filling up your heart.
You love yourself and your heart beats strongly. You spread love to others. We are all connected : We are like a global community.

Affirmation: You have compassion for yourself and others.

Send attention to your heart.

5th BLUE / Throat Chakra

Feel the Blue Bow filling up your throat.
Your voice is heard clearly. You are expressing yourself clearly in all of your relationships. Trust your voice.

Affirmation: I express myself clearly.

Send attention to your throat and neck

6th INDIGO / Brow Chakra

Feel the Indigo Bow filling up your forehead.
You can see through your intuitive mind. You trust your own insights and intuition.

Affirmation: You release any negative thoughts.

Send energy to your forehead and mind.

7th VIOLET / Crown Chakra

Feel the Violet Bow filling up your head.
You feel free within.

Affirmation: You are connected to creation. Send attention to your mind.

Now, gently open your eyes, feel the ground under you.
Feel your body and take a deep breath and stretch.
Keep the good feeling you are feeling right now!

Reiki Energy and Chakra

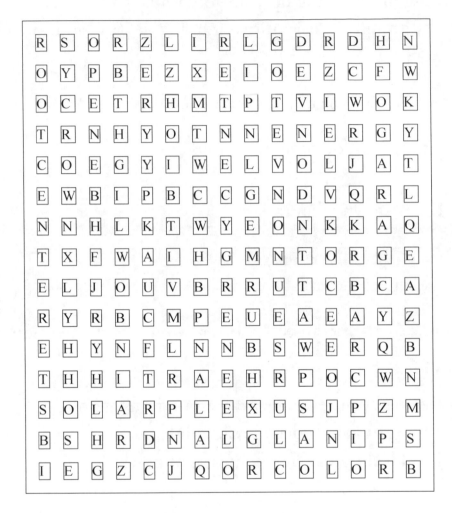

R	O	O	R	Z	L	I	R	L	G	D	R	D	H	N
O	Y	P	B	E	Z	X	E	I	O	E	Z	C	F	W
O	C	E	T	R	H	M	T	P	T	V	I	W	O	K
T	R	N	H	Y	O	T	N	N	E	N	E	R	G	Y
C	O	E	G	Y	I	W	E	L	V	O	L	J	A	T
E	W	B	I	P	B	C	C	G	N	D	V	Q	R	L
N	N	H	L	K	T	W	Y	E	O	N	K	K	A	Q
T	X	F	W	A	I	H	G	M	N	T	O	R	G	E
E	L	J	O	U	V	B	R	R	U	T	C	B	C	A
R	Y	R	B	C	M	P	E	U	E	A	E	A	Y	Z
E	H	Y	N	F	L	N	N	B	S	W	E	R	Q	B
T	H	H	I	T	R	A	E	H	R	P	O	C	W	N
S	O	L	A	R	P	L	E	X	U	S	J	P	Z	M
B	S	H	R	D	N	A	L	G	L	A	N	I	P	S
I	E	G	Z	C	J	Q	O	R	C	O	L	O	R	B

BROWCENTER	COLOR	CROWN
ENERGY	ENERGYCENTER	HEART
LIGHT	LOVE	ONE
OPEN	PEACE	PINALGLAND
POWER	RAINBOW	REIKI
ROOTCENTER	SACRAL	SOLARPLEXUS
THROATCENTER	TOGETHER	WORLD

Tori B. Amos

Making the Healthy Choice

When you make healthy choices in your day, you will have a good day.

Some healthy choices:

- The foods you eat
- Your conversations
- Games you play
- Exercise
- Treating yourself and others with respect
- Meditating
- Speaking positively
- Creating affirmations
- Reiki self-treatments
- Reiki treatments for others, plants and animals
- Hitting the "snooze button" unplugging the
- TV, video games, cell phones, etc.

Put cell phones and electronics to sleep

Activity:

What are some healthy choices you made today, or are going to make tomorrow?

Draw or list _____

ex. Eat a veggie or fruit instead of candy.

Rachael

Caleb and Naima

How else can you give positive energy?
ex. Listen to a friend in need.

_____

Simone

Caleb

What other ways do you unplug?

ex. meditate

Z- Radio
Z-TV

What are some other healthy foods to eat?

ex: Chia seeds / A super food

Charlotte

What are other ways of making healthy choices? "Treating yourself and others with respect?"

Mandala

Mandala means circle in Sanskrit. Sanskrit is an ancient Indic language of India.

Mandalas are used to facilitate meditation and center the body and mind.

Activity:

Color the Mandala. What are some affirmations and or mantras that would be helpful for you right now?

ex: I am safe, because I trust my inner voice.

Growing Your Own Inner Garden

Once you continue to make healthy choices, you are creating healthy "soil," from within to grow your own "inner garden."

Activity:

Q- What does a flower need to grow strong and healthy?
A - Sunlight and healthy soil.

What else could a flower or plant need to grow strong?

_____

Q - What do you need to grow strong and healthy?
A - Healthy food, plenty of water, healthy habits.

What are some other healthy habits?

_____

Q- what does a
flower need to grow?
A- water, sunlight, soil

Q- what does
a kid need
to grow?
A- Healthy
food, water,
Exercise,
Healthy
habits

Elias & Naomi

Feeling Your Own Energy

There are many ways to feel and play with energy. You know when you rub a balloon on your hair and your hair stands up? This is an energy called static electricity.

You learned about the seven main chakras. There are also smaller Chakras in each nerve ending and joints in your body. Your hands alone are "Chak-ra-full" and have 20 joints in them! When you give a high five you are also giving an energetic, "Hello"!

The palm Chakra is the Chakra from which Reiki streams. During a "Reiki Attunement," the palm Chakra and the seven main Chakras receive the Reiki symbols.

Activity:

Rub your palms together quickly 10 times.
What do you feel?
Did they get warm?
Did you feel the energy created between your palms?

Cross Crawl

This exercise is easy to do and it helps you to listen and understand what you are learning.

Put your right hand across your body to the left knee as you raise it and then do the same thing for your left hand on your right knee. This is the same action as if you were marching in place. Notice how you are crossing your body as you do this. Do this exercise for about two minutes or longer.

Hint: It's a good time to use "Cross Crawl" before or during your homework and studying for a test.

Hook Ups

Hook ups are fun! You can use them to feel calm and centered. Cross your right leg over your left ankle. Cross your right wrist over your left wrist and linkup the fingers so that the right wrist is on top. Bend the elbows out and gently turn the fingers in towards the body until they rest in the center of the chest. Stay in this position and breathe evenly for a few minutes.

Hint: It is a good time to use "Hook Ups" when you are upset and want to calm down.

Activity:

Do you know any other activities or techniques for strengthening the body or mind?

_____

Endless River of Abundance

Reiki energy never runs out; it never stops, it is always there. After learning and actually practicing Reiki, you will have a powerful knowledge that you know and own. Chakras, Auras and the way they work are now a part of your understanding! This knowledge that you have learned will never run out, either. With the abundance of your knowledge and your own positive energy, you can accomplish most anything you set your heart and mind to achieving.

In life, there are often times when we need to remain positive. You will need a strong heart and mind to help guide you through some hard times and through good times, as well. As you practice what you have learned, the knowledge you have gained will grow and mature. This is just the start of the positive energy you will feel. Remember, as you practice, your knowledge will continue to grow and it will help to motivate you into creating a momentum that will continue to cultivate other healthy practices in your life.

This knowledge is as powerful as an endless river flowing downstream!

Because you have cultivated this energy into your healthy positive lifestyle, you have earned this healthy endless river of abundance! The more you remember to practice, the more quickly you can engage your positive energy. As long as you keep your healthy practices you will have a life's tool and your positive energy will never run out!

Vocabulary Page

Affirmations - Word or phrases to affirm something. The act or process of being affirmed

Asana – yoga pose

Ashtanga Vinyasa – Flow yoga style

Aura – The distinctive atmosphere or quality that seems to surround and be generated by a person, thing or place. The aura energies surround the physical body and vibrates; so quickly that we can't see them. They are composed of tiny energy lines, like sparkling webs of light that are similar to the lines of a television screen.

Brain Booster- Memory enhancer, intelligence enhancer. Improves mental function.

Chia Seed - Seed found in Mexico dating back to the Mayan and Aztec cultures. Chia means "strength." This super food helps you stay hydrated and lowers blood pressure. Rich in Omega-3 carbohydrates, protein, fiber, antioxidants and calcium.

Chakra - Physical and energetic centers in the human body.

Cross training- training in two or more activities in order to improve performance in a main practice.

Hatha – Physical yoga style

Infinity – Never ending, continuous

Mandala - Circle in Sanskrit. Mandalas are used to facilitate meditation and center the body and mind.

Mantra – " that which protects the mind" and "to free the mind," Words, sounds or phrases repeated to add concentration to a meditation.

The Mind Body Awareness Experience ™ - The cross training of eastern practices, such as meditation, yoga, mantras, mudras energy practices such as Reiki and Qigong. As well as martial arts, healthy diet, mindfulness, respect, the discipline and devotion to make these practices, a part of your daily life…for a lifetime.

Mudra - Symbolic hand gesture

Namaste means -The spirit within me salutes the spirit within you.

Pranayama -Is a Sanskrit word meaning breath.

Qi - An energy force thought to flow through the body.

Qigong - Translated means, life energy cultivation. An energy and breath practice used in some martial arts practices.

Reiki - (Rei- meaning 'spirit') Ki (meaning 'life force energy') Reiki is a Japanese technique of natural hands on healing and positive growth. Reiki always comes from the heart and a loving place. It's an energy that has a positive effect on all living things.

Reiki Attunement - The ceremony when the Reiki Master places the Reiki energy and the Reiki symbols, into the seven main Chakras of the body and into the Chakras of the hands, as well.

Sanskrit - An ancient Indic language of India.

Savasana - Yoga sitting or laying pose.

Taekwondo - One of the world's most popular martial arts. Korean martial art, translated means "the way of the fist foot."

Tai Chi- Chinese system of slow, meditative physical exercise designed for relaxation, balance and health.

Vriksasana - Tree pose, type of yoga pose.

Yin and Yang- Opposing elements thought to make up the universe that needs to be kept in harmony.

Yoga – Means "Binding" or " Union" Yoga is a practice/term, commonly know for physical, mental and spiritual practices or disciplines that originated in ancient India. Yoga's purpose is to attain a state of permanent peace and self- enlightenment.

Yogi - Yoga instructor, person who practices yoga as a lifetime practice.